WESTERN TRAIN ROBBERIES

Don DeNevi

CELESTIAL ARTS
Millbrae, California

Copyright © 1976 by Donald P. DeNevi

CELESTIAL ARTS
231 Adrian Road
Millbrae, California 94030

First Printing, October 1976
Made in the United States of America

Library of Congress Cataloging in Publication Data

DeNevi, Donald P.
 Western train robberies.

1. Train robberies—The West.		I. Title.
HV6658.D45	364.1'55	76-11355
ISBN 0-89087-125-6		

1 2 3 4 5 6 7 — 81 80 79 78 77 76

Contents

This book is dedicated to the greatest of them all . . .

Clarence "Champ" Champlin
Chief Special Agent
Southern Pacific Company

I

The First Western
Train Robbery

So far as popular fancy is concerned, it was Jesse James and a daring band of guerrillas who staged the first train robbery in America on a steamy, hot July afternoon in 1873, in Iowa. But history tells us otherwise. Credit for the first train robbery in the United States belongs to the Reno brothers. Shortly after the close of the Civil War they performed their historical act near Seymour, Indiana. A few weeks later they invaded the county treasurer's office in Gallatin, Missouri, and made off with $20,000. During the years 1867-1869, the Renos robbed the Indianapolis, New Albany, and Jefferson Railroad on a regular basis. After the arrest of his brothers in late 1869, Billy Reno recruited a new gang and continued to successfully rob trains.

The first adventure in robbing trains in the west was initiated by "Gentleman Jack" Davis and his notorious "Seven Knights of the Road" shortly after midnight on November 5th, 1870, in western Nevada. Safely secure in a Wells Fargo Express car on Central Pacific's train Number One, "The Atlantic Express," leaving Oakland, California, for Ogden, Utah, were five strong boxes filled with $41,800 in $20 gold coins and $8,800 in silver bar, along with various bank and commercial drafts. The shiny wood-burning locomotive was pulling two day coaches, a

1

round-ended sleeper, and a combination baggage-express car which carried the payroll shipment for the Comstock miners and other monies of the merchants of Nevada and Utah. As part of a new service on the eighteen-month-old transcontinental line, the Central Pacific routinely diverted payroll cars to Carson and Virginia Cities over the Virginia and Truckee Railroad shuttle.

Because the Comstock mines in the vicinity of Virginia City were in full operation by 1870, large shipments of gold coin were dispatched from San Francisco and Oakland to meet the "Yellow Jacket," "Kentucky," and other Gold Hill mine payrolls during the first few days of each month. It was common knowledge that the shipments were handled by Wells Fargo and Company in the express cars of the Central Pacific Railroad. Few officials cared who knew this fact since such rail shipments were guarded by specially trained agents armed with 16-shot Henry rifles and sawed-off scatter guns. The trains were considered invulnerable.

The fog had been thickening for many days. Now, moving like a gray wall, it fell on Oakland so heavily that it turned the powerful arc-lamps overhead at the small railroad depot into tiny blurs. All but train traffic had ceased and men cursed horribly at the depressing day.

With engineer Hank Small standing at the throttle, the eastbound overland express, pride of the line, ever so slowly inched out of the station in a billow of black smoke for the long haul. As the charcoal cinders settled over the area, no one paid attention to the idle lounger who casually sauntered across the tracks and down Broadway Avenue crowded with immobile horse-buses and vans to Oakland's main telegraph office.

The code name "Red Coat" was used by Wells Fargo and the Central Pacific to designate the Gold Hill payrolls. Exactly how J. E. Chapman, a Sunday School superintendent and leader in the religious life of Reno, Nevada,

The First Western Train Robbery

The Central Pacific's Oakland depot, western
terminus of transcontinental trains

learned the use of the code will never be known. But on
this day when the world seemed to be buried, he used an
alias in sending a telegram to Sol Jones residing in Reno's
popular Capitol House hotel:

> Send me sixty dollars today and charge to my account.
> (signed) J. Enrique

The pious-appearing Chapman had been "Gentleman
Jack's" choice to make the long trip to the Bay Area for the
purpose of finding out when the next payroll shipment
would be made.

Upon receiving the coded message, Sol elatedly spread
the word among his gang of cutthroats, "*Sixty* means
there's sixty thousand dollars on her today, boys. *Today*
means she just pulled out! Two payrolls for sure and all in
gold coin. And it's ours. Let's go!"

One at a time, six bandits casually saddled their horses,
loaded up with arms and ammunition, and rode out of
Reno to an old, deserted mine tunnel in the Peavine

3

J. E. Chapman

Mountains halfway to Verdi, then a rugged logging community 11 miles west of Reno. In the tunnel, they had fashioned a temporary home. Sizeable piles of discarded liquor bottles and refuse indicated this as a regular meeting place. At the entrance, the men had a panoramic view of the razor-straight Central Pacific Railroad tracks below. Two hours before train time, the men would ride from this hideout to Lawton Springs, an old stone quarry on the outskirts of Verdi. There, Sol Jones would take charge of the horses while the other five would return to the Verdi train depot to await the arrival of the train from Sacramento. But now, the men patiently passed the time playing cards, telling jokes, and describing individual plans for spending the sudden wealth.

The engine "C. P. Huntington" on the
Central Pacific tracks near Verdi, Nevada

As the tiny, smoke-belching "puffer" hauling its small string of colorful hotel and commissary cars rumbled out of the orchard fields of the Sacramento Valley up the narrow, zig-zagging grade "over the hill," A. J. "Gentleman Jack" Davis was the last to leave Reno for the abandoned mine tunnel in the isolated clump of hills in the eastern shadow of the Sierras. It was raining heavily now and he hoped there would not be a blizzard before the next morning. Snowslides and deep snowdrifts were particularly dangerous in the area where he would be working.

A. J. "Gentleman Jack" Davis

Davis, once the superintendent of the San Francisco mine at Virginia City and now a professional Comstock mill and ranch owner who raised flowers as a hobby, would never be suspected as the leader of the "Seven Knights of the Road." Gentle, shy, and a patron of the arts, he had the appearance of a mild-mannered college professor or benevolent judge. No other citizen was more warmly welcomed or cultivated in Reno's social circle. He had been

educated in a small eastern university, had traveled exten-
sively, and was an engaging conversationalist. Charismatic
and full of confidence, he looked as if he could turn his
collar around backward and walk into the pulpit of any
church. But when sitting down to a stiff game of low-ball,
opponents quickly forgot his disarming mien as they
watched their hard-earned monies disappear into his
pockets. Surrounded by friends and family, the indepen-
dently wealthy man seemed to enjoy the good, quiet life.

But in reality, it was the treasure-laden stages and
payroll-carrying trains that aroused his imagination. With
the advent of the transcontinental railroad, a death blow
had been struck his prosperous business of stagecoach
robberies. Little by little, the familiar rattle of coach and
chatter of six plunging steeds faded away and left him
little opportunity for adventure and quick gain. Treasures
were now transported by the new carriers of the Central
Pacific, and Wells Fargo trustees breathed sighs of relief. It
had always been tough to guard the slow moving stages.
But not the new locomotives. With "teakettles" puffing
along at 40 miles an hour, it would require the impossible
to rob a train.

As Big Jack arrived darkness was descending, the men
doused their fires with dirt, gathered their dusters, masks,
guns, and ammunition and ambled through the cards, bottles, blankets, and other debris to the tunnel entrance. Big
Jack divided his outlaws—E. B. Parsons, John Squires, Til-
ton Cockerill, R. A. Jones, and James Gilchrist—into two
groups and led them into their final staging area.

With the exception of Davis and Chapman, the men
were fugitives and drifters who mined or gambled for a
living. As part of Reno's floating population, they demonstrated insatiable appetites for gold. And Davis was ready
with the promise of undreamed of wealth. All had proven
their competency, and Gentleman Jack quickly surrounded himself with this staunch gang of brigands.

The reputations of the five were unsavory even in rough

and ready Reno where a man's past or lawless behavior was rarely questioned. Often during the summer of 1870, they were overheard in the bars and bordellos discussing their stage robberies and cattle rustling activities. And, in October, intimate friends were fascinated as they listened while the five quietly debated ways and means of obtaining a train payroll shipment. Pro and con arguments were heard as to whether it would be better to loot the Wells Fargo and Company safe in Reno, where shipments were sometimes stored for transfer by the V. and T. Railroad for Virginia City, or, if a simple, bold holdup of the Central Pacific might have more success.

R. A. Jones

Since nightfall, the heavy rain had been steadily turning to snow as the wood-burning engine followed the rough Truckee River and poked cautiously into the twisting, snowdrifted canyon curves. Ahead was Bill Hill, as train-men called the grade, which climbed steadily for some 7,000 feet before crossing Donner Summit. From there it was downhill all the way into Reno. The trip was cautious and uneventful as Number One chugged up the moun-tainside and looped over the crest. Then, near Truckee, the train was signaled to halt. Ahead was a freight collision which would take a few hours to clear.

Engineer Small was furious at the delay. But since the col-lision caused only momentary delay, the anger turned to one of slight irritation. Now, he felt better as his train gath-ered speed down the eastern slope of the Sierra Nevada.

Through the snow flurries, engineer Small saw the Verdi lights ahead and eased back on his throttle as he rattled over several bridges past the switch points. It was near midnight as the train's whistle rang a clarion note and at reduced speed the locomotive clattered softly through the fledgling village of smoke-filled establishments which offered everything from imported vaudeville to prostitu-tion. A coal-oil headlight provided 30 feet of flickering visibility.

As the light beam passed five squatting figures heavily clothed at the entrance of an abandoned woodshed, they suddenly and silently swung aboard the train, three onto the open front platform of the combination mail-express car behind the tender, two on the back platform of the same car where it coupled onto the first of the day coaches and night sleepers. With linen dusters and black masks pulled over their faces, two men crawled over the wood-pile and dropped into the cab of the engine. With deadly purposefulness, they covered the stunned engineer and sweating fireman with their heavy six-shooters. Without waiting for a fusillade of gunfire, Hank Small at once sur-rendered his engine. While this was going on, the third

9

outlaw climbed over and onto the back of the express car to join the other two who had already taken possession of the rear platform.

Quite unaware that non-paying passengers had boarded, conductor D. G. Marshall casually stepped from the first day coach out onto the open platform on his way to the mail-express car. Three masked men immediately confronted him with their Starr double-action Army .44's leveled at his stomach. Faced with a stern, "Git those Goddam hands up and be quick about it!" and the hardware backing up the command, Marshall abruptly fell back inside the coach, slamming the heavy door shut with his foot.

In the meantime, while the train continued to gather momentum a few miles east of Verdi, a bandit in the engine cab shoved a gun into Small's ribs and ordered him to "whistle off the brakes." Air brakes had not been invented yet and the engineer had to pull off one short blast of the whistle in order to bring the brakemen to their respective platforms where they would quickly begin the work of bringing the mass of iron, steel, and wood to a halt. But the whistle was also planned to signal the other robbers at the rear of the express car platform to sever the bell-rope and pull the coupling-pin.

Hearing the whistle, Marshall hesitated for a minute in the coach. "Brakes?" he fumed. "What the Hell is going on?" With anger rapidly rising within him, he grabbed a fire axe off the rear wall of the Silver Palace day coach and rushed toward the platform where the bandits had been. Bursting onto the forward platform, the conductor found that his non-paying passengers had escaped, taking the locomotive, tender, and mail-express car with them! While the conductor hesitated during those 60 seconds, the train had been halted and swift fingers pulled the link-pin coupling the mail express and coaches. Now, the severed end of the signal cord that linked the cars together whipped aimlessly in the falling snow. He watched in stunned amazement as the engine with its two cars trailing behind began to roar down the tracks cutting along snow-covered sage brush, behind a picture of curling snow wreaths. The rest of the train upon which Marshall was standing rolled quietly to a halt in the night.

With the engineer and fireman ordered to "give her full steam," the train bellowed and clamored through the evening stillness. At a point six or seven miles beyond Verdi, Small was commanded to stop again—this time at the Lawton Springs gravel quarry where Sol Jones waited

The Lawton Springs stone quarry and Central Pacific tracks on the outskirts of Verdi, Nevada

with eight horses. During the idle hours before the hijacking, Jones had carefully piled rail ties on the tracks to insure the train stopping at the designated spot. The engineer might get a bright idea about resisting. Indeed, for a few moments, Small thought of releasing the full throttle

11

and jumping, but the cold muzzle of the .44 against his temple brought him back to reality.

With the engine crunching to a halt, an articulate and pleasant-voiced bandit who remained in the background during the activity now took command. He quickly herded Small and his terrified fireman down from the cab to the express car door and knocked. Closeted within the combination mail-express Wells Fargo car, Frank Minchell, the Central Pacific messenger, found nothing unusual in the train's recent stop-and-go pattern. He attributed the jerking to the train's frequent mechanical failures or perhaps some tree branches that had fallen on the tracks during the storm.

"Is that you, conductor?" asked the messenger, looking at his watch and thinking the train had arrived in Reno.

"No, it's me, Hank Small, the engineer," was the sullen reply.

Without bothering to pick up his Winchester .44 from the corner of his cubicle, Minchell opened the inside lock bolt and shoved the sliding door wide. The muzzles of three double-barreled, sawed-off shotguns faced him in the flickering light of the lanterns. "Hold it!" snarled one of the bandits. Taken completely by surprise, he raised his hands. The pleasant-voiced man advised him to face the inside wall of the car and remain quiet. Any hasty movements would automatically bring death. Then, the bandit ordered Small and the fireman to join Minchell.

With an oath, Small sulkily obeyed. With the way now clear, the outlaws could loot the padlocked treasure boxes at will. Sol Jones ran up with crowbars and other prying tools to wrench open the bolts of the chests. Efficiently and without discussion, they broke open the boxes and ransacked the contents. One bandit smashed a small sack of coins against the edge of a safe, bursting it so that silver dollars spilled everywhere. Disgustedly, he disregarded the money. The outlaws wanted only gold. While Gentleman Jack carefully piled up sacks of gold coin at the car's

One of the five Wells, Fargo & Co. treasure
boxes filled with $20 gold pieces

gaping doorway, the other bandits went to work on other
locked drawers and safes, searching mail pouches and
other bags and envelopes.

Within an hour, the men had loaded over $41,000 in
$20 gold pieces into the bags on the eight horses. They
discarded $8,500 in bar silver and silver dollars as being
too heavy to carry and totally ignored hundreds of bank
drafts and other commercial papers. After inspecting the
car to make sure no clues were left behind, the pleasant-
voiced leader ordered the men to retreat in their separate

13

directions. Gentleman Jack then turned to the three Central Pacific and Wells Fargo employees still facing the wall with their hands up and thanked them for giving so little trouble, adding that he personally was glad the gang did not have to resort to homicidal means. Shouldering the messenger's Winchester and his share of the booty, he disappeared into the snow flurries. Unknown to Davis, he was leaving over $15,000 in gold bars which had been hidden under the firewood next to the express car's heating stove. A few moments later, Small with his fireman and messenger got up steam, pouring cord after cord of wood into the devouring firebox.

After Small had his firebox roaring, he and the two others quickly removed the obstructions from the tracks. Reversing the engine, he returned to Verdi to recouple the cars. From there he tried to send a telegram to Nels Hammond, the Wells Fargo special agent in Reno, but realized the telegraph wires had been cut in several places. Thus, it was near dawn before the diamond-stacked brass engine pulled into the Reno station to alarm officials with news of the staggering loss. Within hours, half of Reno turned out to inspect the barren express car.

The first western train robbery had been accomplished in less than two hours just a little after midnight on Saturday morning, November 5, 1870, and not a shot had been fired. Sheriff Calvin Pegg of Washoe County was thunderstruck. The sheer effrontery of the whole affair was conducted in such a well-organized and polished manner that a great debate immediately broke out among his deputies as to the culprits' identities.

Sheriff Pegg and Undersheriff James Kinkead immediately formed a posse of fourteen available men. The snow flurries had now turned into a light, chilly rain when the men began saddling up and struck for the Sierra Nevada mountains. Pegg's information had been that the brigands were headed south from *between* Truckee and the Verdi, and he hoped to head them off later in the after-

James H. Kinkead

noon. In the meantime, every other exit out of the region was ordered closed and guarded.

It wasn't long before they discovered what they thought was a trail. Following it northerly for a few miles the trail began to fade and Pegg and his posse returned to Washoe City, south of Reno, convinced it was erroneous. Actually the wire Pegg received was misleading since the robbery occurred between Verdi and *Reno* instead of Truckee. Meanwhile, deputies throughout Nevada were stopping all travelers on every path, road, and trail for questioning.

Later that afternoon telegraphs flashed around the world and created quite a sensation: Newspapers head-lined that Nevada had the dubious distinction of having the first western train robbery in history. Not only did it signal things to come in the corporate minds of Wells Fargo and Central Pacific, but it also reached deeply into the civic consciences of Nevada's pioneers. Wells Fargo and Company immediately offered a $10,000 reward while the Central Pacific Railroad and the State of Nevada each contributed $15,000, bringing the total to $40,000 for the gang—the largest reward ever offered in the West.

That evening the San Francisco *Daily Alta* wasted no time in carrying an editorial on the front page which read in part:

> This affair has struck everybody with amazement, so bold, decisive, well planned and successful has it proved. An end must be quickly put to this still neophyte form of banditry before others imitate it—devil-may-care desperadoes flaunting long-barreled revolvers in stealing mail of yours and mine.

And because a romantic myth of daring was likely to spring up overnight, it was imperative the bandits be caught. Therefore, Wells Fargo and Central Pacific decided to assign the veteran and redoubtable detective, F. T. Burke, to the investigation. Both companies agreed to jointly share manpower and expense in tracking down the gang. Within 24 hours, Burke was dispatched from San Francisco and arrived in Verdi on a special flyer to link up with sheriff Pegg's posse waiting for him at Verdi.

Early the next morning in the continuing light rain, the heavily armed group rode from Verdi to the scene of the robbery. Burke carefully examined the ground, the silver coins, the remains of the Wells Fargo treasure chests, the crowbars and picks used to pry open the locks and hinges. But the important discovery was of one footprint, easily distinguished from the others, not totally washed away. It was made by a boot having a very small and unusual heel. Few men, and certainly no railroad employee ever wore such a shoe. A hundred yards down the grade that heel-print and two larger ones left the track and led off to the north. The robbers had evidently walked for quite a distance on the railroad ties to prevent being trailed, hoping the snow and rain would wash out their footprints. They then mounted their horses and fled in a northerly direction up into the Sierras. Burke, Pegg, and the posse followed the quick-fading horse tracks in the snow up Dog Valley Creek and to Pearson's Tavern in Sardine Valley, California. Cold, weary, and depressed, the group filed into the boardinghouse saloon, a primitive two-story structure catering to drifters. What they heard from the proprietor quickly brought them back to their senses.

Three heavily laden strangers had stumbled into the tavern the night before and immediately pulled off their boots and warmed their feet at the stove. After consuming several bottles of expensive whiskey, they ordered a huge supper which they devoured. Finishing it, they asked for overnight lodging, paying the innkeeper with three $20 gold pieces. Then they carried their bulging saddlebags to their rooms and promptly fell asleep on the bunks without taking their clothes off. Although innkeeper Pearson was delighted that business was booming at this time of year, Mrs. Pearson's imagination was aroused. Who were these hungry beasties with darkened faces and bloodshot eyes paying and throwing around goldpieces at five times the normal rate for room and board?

Unable to sleep that night, she heard squeaking floorboards from above at 2:00 a.m. She woke her husband who also heard muffled conversation and men preparing to leave. But since they had paid their bill, he thought they simply might be getting an early start to wherever they were going. Annoyed, he told his wife to shut up and go back to sleep. But she strained her ears at the conversations and once thought she heard the words "gold cache." Finally, she heard two men descend the tavern stairs and ride away, she dozed off.

Early the next morning, the third man wearily ambled down to breakfast. Staring blankly at the tablecloth between mouthfuls of bacon and scrambled eggs, he was in

17

no mood for conversation. He was obviously exhausted from some previous exertion. His matted hair hung tangled over a wrinkled face. Sullenly eyeing Mrs. Pearson who was serving his coffee, he said, "Guess I'll sleep over another day. I'm dead tired from stumbling through the snow."

Mrs. Pearson's curiosity knew no bounds as she watched the dejected man suddenly lose interest in his breakfast and rise from the table. Making a rather hurried exit from the dining room, he climbed the stairs to his room and locked the door. Mrs. Pearson didn't hesitate to follow. From the entrance of the tavern, she circled around in the snow to the backstairs. Without any hesitation, she slipped up the stairs to the second floor and tiptoed down the hall to room 15. Quickly she bent down and placed her eye to the door and looked through the small keyhole. She almost fell down as she incredulously watched the man pour $20 goldpieces from a large saddlebag into several smaller pocket bags. Then, she watched as the man hobbled to his bunk and collapsed.

Trembling with excitement, Mrs. Pearson hurried down to tell her husband what she had seen. Although doubting his wife, the innkeeper nonetheless sent two boarders for the deputy sheriff stationed at Dog Valley Creek. Then, he warned his wife to barricade herself in their own living quarters and remain there until he deemed it safe for her to come out. After all, this man might not only be a thief, but a killer. Grabbing his double-barreled shotgun, he laid it across his lap as he sat at the main desk playing solitaire.

With the arrival of the posse, the landlady cooperated fully. According to a plan laid out by Burke, she knocked on the bandit's door. Aroused, he walked across the room mumbling to himself. When he answered, he flushed as he looked into the muzzles of several rifles and pistols leveled at his head. Safely handcuffed, the man proved to be James Gilchrist, a dull-witted mining fetcher-and-carrier from Virginia City who had never been in serious trouble

James Gilchrist

with the law before. Tearing off a piece of tobacco in his yellow teeth, he affected an air of casualness as he explained this was his first venture in the "hold-up" business. Looking aslant at Pegg, his coarse voice assumed a wheedling tone as he described his saddle activities over deep snow-drifts.

Now, watching two lawmen carry his share of the loot down the stairs and out the tavern, he cursed the nosey old bitch. Realizing the bandit was a mediocre man, Burke and Pegg decided to be neither kind nor patient. Pegg casually mentioned that a "hangman's party" was waiting for the dastardly coward who would dare perpetrate the first train robbery in western America and smirch the honor of hardworking pioneers. Soon, Gilchrist shook his head and started pleading for his life.

"Where's your friends?" Pegg demanded.

Gilchrist's heavy brows dropped low.

"Listen!" shouted the sheriff, raising a warning hand, "you're a dead man in a few hours. You better talk and talk awfully Goddam fast!"

Members of the posse were all silently watching the exchange. Gilchrist's face had lost a bit of its swarthy color and the lines about his mouth hardened. Finally, he blurted:

"I'm a loyal man. But, I can't traffic my own hanging."

Gilchrist sat down, and motioned Pegg, Kinkead, and Burke to join him. He then unfolded the whole story.

The manhunters learned that it was "Gentleman Jack" Davis who masterminded the robbery with Chapman, alias "Joseph Enrique." And it was Davis who took the lion's share of the take, $22,500, while the other six divided the remainder among themselves. After the robbery, each man was on his own. If he chose to bury his share in a separate cache, that was his business; if he wanted to ride along, he could. Or, if he decided to join a group, it was his decision. As far as Gilchrist knew, Davis hastily mounted his horse after the robbery and rode away with several of his leather gripsacks filled with double-eagles. With Sol Jones and Tilton Cockerill disappearing together, he decided to throw in with John Squires and E. B. Parsons. With the loot divided on the spot, no one person knew where the others were going unless he joined their group. Squires had planned all along to head for his brother's ranch in Loyalton, California. After the robbery, Squires led Parsons and Gilchrist through the heavy timber that clothed the summit of the Sierra Nevada to the alpine tavern in Sardine Valley.

By resting in Pearson's warm beds for an evening, they would be ready the next morning to forge up the same mountains which some twenty years earlier had brought tragedy to the emigrant Donner party. Winding over to California in that manner they would be sure to lose possible trackers. Gilchrist complained that he had never suffered such a hard, damp, and dangerous journey. Ploughing through snowdrifts, gorges yawned below them; above them, the inaccessible flank of the mountain. The snow covered ravines darkened and the foliage had met above their heads by the time they reached Pearson's tavern.

Gilchrist then gave the officers a complete description of the other two heavily armed bandits. John Squires wore a "gambler's boot," and from his description of the other man, Pegg guessed that he was an old stage robber whom the officers of Storey County had been trying to catch for years. Gilchrist explained the two were now heading toward a small hamlet in Loyalton in Sierra Valley, where Squire's brother Joe, an honest blacksmith, lived. From there, it would be a short hop to Grass Valley, where there was a small ranch to hide out for several months.

While the posse fed and rested their horses which they had been riding since daylight, Pegg clapped Gilchrist in irons and wired captain Clarke of the Virginia City Police to arrest "Gentleman Jack" Davis and Chapman when he returned from Oakland, Calif. At 11:00 p.m. that night, and with another heavy snow falling, Burke, Pegg, and his officers headed for Loyalton. Pegg, however, was now out of his arresting jurisdiction and unacquainted with that mountainous section of California. The posse needed a guide to Loyalton, otherwise they might wind up at Webber Lake, or even Downieville. But since none of the other boarders had "lost any robbers," they politely refused to act as guides.

However, a fourteen-year-old boy volunteered for a $20 gold piece and Burke gladly paid in advance. But, the young fellow added one stipulation: in case the lawmen encountered the bandits, he would immediately turn back and let the posse shoot it out alone.

Toiling through blind snow and near zero temperatures, the officers arrived on the outskirts of the small village of Loyalton early the next morning. Arousing the sleeping landlord of the only hotel in town, Burke asked if any strange guests had checked in during the night. The landlord angrily replied that only one man had come in and he was upstairs on the third floor in Room 21. Although the man's description did not match either of the two men sought, Burke and Pegg figured it would be best to check him out anyway. Sensing there might be gunplay, the landlord offered them a candle, pointed the way, and quickly retired to his room.

Since the three-story hotel had just been built and not yet painted, the door to Room 21 was swollen from the freezing weather. It could not be shut tight enough to lock. As Burke and Pegg climbed the stairs and advanced down the hall, they noticed the occupant had crudely placed a small chair under the knob on the inside of the room and had gone to bed.

Gently, Burke pushed the door until the chair moved sufficiently for him to stretch his arm through the crack and quietly remove the obstructing chair. The man continued to snore heavily in the makeshift bunk. Burke's attention was immediately attracted by a boot lying on the floor near the bed. That boot had an unusually small heel. It was a "gambler's boot."

With Winchesters and double-barreled shotguns raised, the entire posse entered the room. Covered by Pegg and the others, Burke gently removed a loaded six-shooter the snoring man had under his pillow. The two officers then searched his clothes for more incriminating evidence.

When Burke finally roused the slumberer, the man bounded from his bed in a state of shock. He leaped back for his gun under the pillow. Finding it missing, he simply raised his arms. Pegg commanded the bandit to put on his clothes and march down the hotel stairs to the entrance where he was bound and placed under guard. The man turned out to be Parsons, a small-time gambler from Virginia City. Pegg learned from the innkeeper that Squires' brother had his ranch a few miles down the road.

With Parsons double-chained, the posse continued on toward the ranch. It was nearing six a.m. and snow was still falling heavily.

The posse found the small farm without difficulty and immediately began encircling it. Pegg knew of Squires' reputation and confided to Burke that there would be trouble in taking him "in the open." They prepared for a possible siege as soon as it became light enough.

Although nearly frozen and totally exhausted, they waited in silent watchfulness, each man alert, rifles unslung, revolvers loose in holsters. Burke stationed himself at the rear of the house, while Pegg and his men flanked the road and zigzag fence. Two men slipped into the snow-covered willows in front.

They didn't have to wait long. At 6:45 a.m., a man ambled through the kitchen carrying a pail and left the door ajar on his way to the barn. He was on his way for some morning milk.

Burke motioned to Pegg and immediately slipped into the house through the open kitchen door. The detective found nine slumbering men in four separate rooms before he spotted Squires. In the meantime, the posse infiltrated the house, stationing themselves at various strategic positions with shotguns raised.

Again Burke had the good luck to disarm a bandit without waking him. Gathering up the man's clothes and boots, he aroused him with the muzzle of his rifle and forced him out of the house where he was allowed to dress.

Suddenly, the milkman emerged from the barn to see what was going on in the yard. A noisy crowd was quickly developing from nearby houses and farms. After tying his third prisoner up, Sheriff Pegg delivered an impromptu speech to the restive crowd of 20 explaining that he was an officer of the peace discharging his duty. He was arresting

Squires on suspicion of complicity in the Verdi train robbery. If anyone resisted, he would be considered an accomplice. Squires laughed. Recognizing Pegg and the posse, he claimed that Nevada deputies had no right to make an arrest in California. Joe Squires, his brother, concurred. Since Joe was a popular and respectable citizen in the valley and all in the crowd were his friends, Pegg started to get nervous. A team was quickly hitched up. It looked bad for the party. When the buckboard was ready and waiting in the rear of a nearby cafe, the shackled bandit was rushed onto it by the posse and Burke succeeded in getting him away without further trouble. Later that morning, Squires and Parsons were confined in separate cells in the Truckee jail.

From the Truckee telegraph office, Burke wired H. G. Blasdel, the governor of Nevada, to send a requisition to Governor Haight of California for the extradition of the two train robbers. Late that evening the extradition order arrived and the bandits were transported under heavy guard across the state line into Nevada. Ironically, it was over the same railroad whose train they had assisted in holding up.

Unknown to Squires, Gilchrist had been "sweated" to make a complete confession before a Notary Public. Squires was stunned to learn the posse now had the names of all the conspirators. Even before Gilchrist and Squires arrived in Reno, Davis was locked behind bars. Jones and Cockerell were captured in a bordello in Long Valley by a 28-man posse headed by chief Burke of Sacramento and Louis Dean of Reno. When arrested, all the men had their loot with them. Chapman arrived from Oakland the following day, and was arrested by deputy sheriff Edwards as he unobtrusively stepped from the night sleeper.

Within four days of the Verdi holdup, the "Seven Knights of the Road" were locked safely behind bars.

$39,750 of the gold coins were recovered. Where the remaining $3,000 was cached by either Davis or Sol Jones was never discovered and to this day there is speculation it remains buried either at the site of the robbery or in the vicinity of the abandoned mine tunnel.*

A grand jury was immediately called by Judge C. N. Harris of the district court of Washoe County and the bandits were formally arraigned on November 12. Bail was set for $20,000 apiece. And even Gentleman Jack couldn't afford that.

When the robbers came to trial in early December, they learned that it was Gilchrist who had turned state's evidence and was now free. The remaining six had little defense against his complete confession except for the unique plea they had been driven to the cowardly deed because they had been unable to hold up a stage for quite awhile!

The trial was a memorable one in the criminal annals of Nevada. A great legal battle developed around Davis, the debonaire Comstock rancher-businessman hitherto unsuspected of anything but civic rectitude and a little gambling now and then. He was respected by lawyers, bankers, businessmen, judges, and other Reno dignitaries, although there was no doubt in anyone's mind that he was the brains behind the gang's operations.

It was revealed during the trial that no one could remember any ore ever being brought to his mill or indeed ever seeing a single ore wagon in the vicinity. The prosecution charged that he had leased the mill so he could remelt, remold and market the bullion obtained in his various holdups. But in order to avoid going to prison, Davis

---

*If a patient treasure hunter were to find the small hoard of 150 coins, he would be in for an extra surprise. Those $20 gold pieces were minted in San Francisco and sent to Wells Fargo through a Montgomery Street Bank. Today collector pricelists value each coin at over $300 apiece . . . or $450,000.

quietly and rationally fought desperately against the state's prosecutors and the attorneys specially employed by Wells Fargo and Central Pacific. His brilliant mind was not dulled by the exigencies of the occasion. Indeed, he alertly maneuvered the Wells Fargo attorney to quarrel with his own special agent, detective Burke, on various facts and points of law. Gentleman Jack also received support from his respectable friends and associates. Indeed, it appeared he was going to be set free until a federal agent threatened to prosecute him for stopping the mail if the state didn't do its duty.

On December 23, the jury arrived at six counts of guilty for all the defendants and Judge Harris handed down five 21-year sentences on the rockpiles of the Nevada State prison at Carson City. In Gentleman Jack's case, Judge Harris limited the sentence to a mere ten years without explanation. In any event, all six arrived together in the same van to begin their sentences on Christmas Eve of 1870.

A few years after Davis' incarceration there occured a bloody escape attempt from the Nevada State Prison. Several guards were killed and the warden held hostage by 70 inmates. Although the convicts had complete control of the prison, Davis refused to participate. Rather than pass through the open gates, he offered some assistance to the officers. From the first day of his incarceration his conduct had been submissive and orderly and he wasn't about to risk an early parole for a feebleminded escape attempt. After the riot was quelled, Gentleman Jack was pardoned. But within a year after his discharge he foolishly attempted single-handedly to hold up the stage between Tybo and Eureka in White Pine County. Eugene Blair, a shotgun messenger who boasted he had never lost a battle, riddled the pleasant-voiced bandit with a load of buckshot. "By God, I made a truly good John out of him!" he told newspaper reporters. Thus did the man with the courteous gestures ignominiously pass into history.

II

The Daltons Whirl Westward

Silence hung heavy late one afternoon in the sleepy Southern Pacific station of Alila in California's San Joaquin Valley. Suddenly, there came the rumble and roar of southbound passenger No. 17, shattering the warm stillness with sharp echoes. As a few lounging railroad workmen opened their eyes blinkingly and then turned away with stolid indifference, a depot agent sauntered out of a low adobe building and waited for the creaking, clattering Los Angeles bound locomotive to grind to a halt.

"Too bad they can't give a man a clear line when he's running a string like this on passenger time," the greasy, sweating engineer shouted down from his cab.

"Well, we have passengers too, you know, even though we're a one-horse freight yard," laughed the depot manager.

"I just hope there are no more red-eyes before we get to Bakersfield," grumbled the fireman as he leaned out the gangway.

Alila was only a cattleyard station, a shipping point for the mighty spreads of rolling plains which make up the lower San Joaquin. Aside from the post office, it had two saloons, a store, a boarding house or two, and the low station house.

The Valley Springs station near Visalia

A few minutes after several passengers and cowboys clambered aboard with their packages and weathered suitcases, the crack express slowly rumbled out of the station and past a string of empty boxcars basking in the sun. Dancing between the tender and firebox as the locomotive began to gain momentum, fireman Ivy Radcliffe noticed a man racing from one of the boxcars toward him. The man was obviously too active for a hobo or tramp and he seemed most anxious to board.

At that moment, two masked men crawled over the wood tender to the cab from the gangway of the mail-express car.

"All right, hold it!" shouted a tall, masked man pointing his revolver at the two stunned crewmen. While the third man clambered aboard, engineer Joseph P. Thorne and fireman Ernest Radcliff observed two armed men standing before them in striking contrast. One stood with his feet

28

well apart, sinews pulled tight like a wirerope over his tall, thin frame, his face obviously swarthy although partly hidden by a red bandana mask, hair tinged with gray, and steady blue eyes. Two fingers were gone from the steady hand holding the Remington Frontier .44 and there was a deep hole in his right cheek which quivered grotesquely as he spoke. The other bandit was smaller, but with broader shoulders. Bent with obvious fatigue and begrimed with dirt, the man's black eyes nonetheless flashed with the unsubdued fire of youth. He wore a small white handkerchief with a hole cut in it, for a mask.

The two outlaws now stared vaguely at the crewmen for a few seconds, allowing the puffing and coughing third bandit to catch his breath. Then the tall bandit said, "All right! Light your pipe, old man, and settle down for a nice smoke. We'll watch the signals and switches. Shift the lever a notch to regulate the throttle a little. We'll tell you when we want you to stop. You just keep waving at the crossing-tenders or the tower-men along the way."

The engineer released the lever and sat down on his chair near the cab window. The fireman gave the fire a little wood, shut the firebox door and glumly sat down on an empty box next to his fire.

The 8000, with straight track under her drivers and the throttle open, "pounded the joints" as it steamed through the broad San Joaquin Valley. Passing isolated farmhouses and crossing several bridges, the train chugged along for seventeen miles. The sides of the valley were beginning to close in and become steeper when the tall bandit ordered the engineer to bring the train to a halt. Orange flames flickered from the huge firebox. The sun was descending in a ball of red in the west and the engineer could hear frogs croaking in nearby ponds.

The engine crew was then ordered to climb down the cab and walk back to the express car and order messenger Charles C. Haswell to open up. But when the train had made the sudden stop, the messenger immediately slipped

29

The Southern Pacific's "8000" steaming
through the San Joaquin Valley

his watch from his pocket. They weren't due to reach Delano for another 30 minutes. He slid open the door of his mail car to find out what the trouble was. Bending his eyes down the rails, he observed the engineer and fireman leaving the engine followed by three masked men. He bolted the heavy door shut and grabbed his Winchester .44-40 rifle and revolver ready for action. He then ran over to the rear door of the car. At that moment, he saw the head brakeman casually walking from the passenger cars to determine the cause of the delay. When the brakeman noticed that three of the men near the mailcar were wearing masks, he started to retreat. A man raced forward and shouted to him to stop or he would fire. The brakeman stopped and respectfully raised his hands.

As the engineer, fireman, and brakeman were quickly

marched to the door of the express car, Haswell extinguished the interior light and resumed his post at the rear door.

"Open up," shouted one of the bandits. "It's me, the engineer!"

"I'll see you in Hell first!" shouted the messenger. When he turned to look out through this window, he saw a shotgun pointed toward him. At the moment he instinctively dodged back, the shotgun was fired at point-blank range. Miraculously, he was not killed although one of the pellets struck him in the left eye, causing Haswell to bleed profusely. White with rage, he returned the fire. Haswell then stumbled to the forward end of the car and grabbed a double-barreled shotgun off the rack. He planned to use it through the grating in the lower part of the door.

For a moment there was deadly silence. Then a vicious battle exploded with the popping and cracking of rifles, shotguns, and revolvers. It lasted no longer than two or three minutes ending as suddenly as it began, the messenger had won a tremendous victory by beating back the heavily armed bandits who then fled on horseback. In the robbers' attempt to kill Haswell, twenty-six holes had been shot into the express car. But during the fight, fireman Radcliff, who had been standing beside the express car, was shot in the stomach and died instantly. Hearing the terrific roar of gun fire, conductor Bill Morris swung from the rear platform of the caboose to investigate. But no sooner had he cautiously made his way half way up the train when the brakeman raced toward him reporting that the fireman had been killed. All the passengers were in wild confusion. The amount of promiscuous shooting was unprecedented. Men and women were hiding their valuables wherever they could.

When the details of the holdup became known, Haswell was a popular hero overnight. Because of his splendid resistance, the town of Delano was in a frenzy of excitement. But his heroism was soon dimmed by the charge that it was he who had shot and killed Radcliff. Even though it was accidental, the labor organization to which Radcliff belonged pressed charges and sentiment quickly turned against him. Within a few days after the holdup, a grand jury in Visalia indicted the wounded messenger for the shooting of his colleague. Popular opinion was divided whether indeed he had, but popular excitement couldn't have been higher.

In the trial that took place within a week of the robbery, Haswell, testifying in his own defense, stated that when the gunfight began, one of the robbers was on the opposite side of the mail car from where Radcliff was standing. This bandit was attempting to kill him by shooting through the floor of the car with a Winchester rifle. The lower part of the car was examined, and indeed bore marks which substantiated Haswell's testimony. The messenger's theory was that it was one of the bullets fired by this bandit that killed Radcliff accidentally. An autopsy revealed that the bullet that struck the fireman entered the stomach and ranged upward. Since Haswell was shooting from up above, it was impossible for a bullet from his gun to cause such a wound. With a diagram of the mail car showing the position of the grating five feet above the track, the messenger made his point cogently and concisely. Other witnesses, including the train crew, gave similar testimony which finally resulted in Haswell's acquittal.

But who were the desperadoes? Why had they abandoned the attempt to rob the train so quickly? Had one of them been wounded? Why hadn't they used demolition devices?

B. F. Whitmer, the Southern Pacific special agent, told a reporter of the Fresno *Expositor:*

> I don't think the fact of their having been excited and frightened is a good argument in favor of the supposition that the robbers were new at the business. They stopped the train on an isolated stretch and expected to have things

all their own way. The strenuous defense by the messenger surprised them. Then they had good reason to believe that the fusillade which followed would be heard by farmers near by. So they did not wish to run the risk of being captured by persisting in the undertaking.

In the meantime, posses were organized at Tulare and Visalia and over 150 men were pressed into service. Over forty men under Sheriff Vern Borgwaldt of Kern County arrived at the scene of the robbery attempt within hours on a special train from Bakersfield. Sheriff John Kay of Tulare County also arrived at the scene shortly after the holdup. The next morning the two posses began searching the vicinity and it wasn't long before they found the bandits' camp. Around a smoldering fire, they discovered parts of a lunch, rosettes from bridles, two pieces of stirrups with pieces of sheepskin tied at the corners, a number of leather strings, and two tapaderos. The trail led toward the Pacific Coast Range.

The two posses fanned out and followed the trail over the mountains to the little village of Huron in San Luis Obispo County. Descriptions were easily obtained from several witnesses who had seen four heavily armed men in the neighborhood traveling toward the San Joaquin Valley a few days before. And, it was learned from a rancher that men answering the descriptions had been seen on the trail near his ranch house on their way deeper into the mountains the day after the holdup. The two groups of manhunters conferred and then split up as they hastened into the mountains. With Sheriff Borgwaldt in command of the posses combing the valleys, canyons, and the mountain caves and peaks, Sheriff Kay and two men returned to Visalia to announce the train robbers were surrounded.

County officers now assisted by Southern Pacific and Wells Fargo detectives began to analyze the articles found at the scene of the crime. It was learned that the portions of the lunch were similar to a lunch which had been prepared by a restaurant man at Delano, eight miles from the scene of the holdup. On checking the other articles, it was discovered that the saddle parts were borrowed from a neighbor by William Dalton, who had a ranch in the

The State Pacific Coast Railroad at Los Olivos station. William Dalton's ranch was located in the background a few miles away

mountains of San Luis Obispo County. Although worn and weary members of the posse began drifting back to Visalia empty-handed after a week of searching, the trail now led back in the direction they had come. But this time it included one of the most notorious names in the criminal annals of the West.

Suspicion fell on the Dalton brothers.

Cousins of the Younger brothers, friends of the James boys, the Daltons grew up outside the sleepy settlement of Coffeyville, Kansas, where their kinsmen and the James'

34

were local celebrities. Forming a gang of their own in 1889, the Dalton brothers were involved in cattle rustling, horse stealing, stage, bank, and train robberies, and cold-blooded murder. No outlaw band operating in the United States established a worse record as it roamed the Midwest without challenge, robbing and killing at will.

And now they were in California.

Sheriffs Borgwald and Kay learned that Robert and Emmett Dalton had been seen around William Dalton's ranch for some time and their habit of always carrying weapons had caused comment. The descriptions of the Dalton brothers fitted the descriptions of the bandits, as well as of the persons seen on the trail leading from the scene of the holdup to Huron.

Neighbors said that Robert and Emmett Dalton had arrived in California as early as October 1890, and headed straight to the ranch in the mountains operated by their brother William eleven miles from Paso Robles. Both Robert and Emmett were being vigorously sought on seven indictments for horse stealing and murder at Fort Smith, Arkansas. Grattan Dalton became involved in a shooting scrape in the Indian Territory while acting as a deputy marshal, and left that vicinity when a United States commissioner's warrant was issued for his arrest. Although he arrived at William's ranch on January 15, 1891, Grattan was familiar with this section of the country since he had visited California a couple of years before.

Further interviews with nearby ranchers and farmers revealed that Robert, Grattan, Emmett, and William left the ranch on January 28, on horseback in the direction of the San Joaquin Valley. It was then discovered that while the others remained in the burgs of Tulare and Traver, Emmett had gone by train to Oakland in order to learn the exact date a Wells Fargo money shipment was to be made to Los Angeles. Obtaining the desired information, he sent a coded message to his brothers and then rode the train to the scene of the holdup. Supposedly, he disembarked from a passenger car at Alila and joined a brother at the gangway to the tender. Haswell suggested it was Emmett who shot Radcliffe from under the express car.

An immediate reward was offered for the arrest and conviction of the four Daltons. On February 12, less than a week after the robbery attempt, P. J. Conway, who operated a saloon-cafe in Tulare, recognized Grattan Dalton from a poster he had seen on Fresno Street. Exercising his right as a citizen, Conway placed him under arrest for the train robbery. With people all around, Dalton offered no resistance. He was immediately taken to the county jail in Visalia and questioned by detective Smith of the Southern Pacific, detective Hume of Wells Fargo, and Sheriff Kay. After a brief and disappointing statement had been secured from him, it was agreed there was not sufficient evidence to hold him. Reluctantly, he was released.

On investigating Grattan's story, the officers found several discrepancies. But a few days later, when detective Hickey of the Southern Pacific identified the stirrups, tapaderos, and pieces of sheepskin found at the scene of the campsite as having been loaned to William Dalton by a neighbor, detective Smith and Sheriff E. F. O'Neill of San Luis Obispo County rode out to William's ranch and re-arrested Grattan.

A week later, the grand jury of Tulare County returned an indictment charging Robert and Emmett Dalton with assault with intent to commit train robbery and William with harboring known criminals.

After his arrest, William Dalton confessed he had taken his brothers to a safe hiding place, but denied any of them had participated in the Alila holdup. He stated he had assisted them to hide, because they were wanted for murder in the Midwest.

Now, bargaining with the officers, William said he could induce Bob and Emmett to surrender, if the sheriffs would guarantee that his brothers would not be extradited, and if they would allow him to go alone to persuade

Robert Dalton

Grattan Dalton

William Dalton

Emmett Dalton

his brothers to surrender. The sheriffs had a good laugh at that, and then refused to enter into any such agreement. With William locked away, they vigorously continued the search. But Robert and Emmett had fled, heading into the Sierra Nevadas after which they made their way back to Kansas.

In Visalia, William Dalton was released on $300 bail. Well liked in the area, he had the best reputation of the brothers. Indeed, he dabbled in politics and was on the verge of running for assemblyman. Grattan was brought to trial in the superior court of Tulare County on the charge of assault with intent to hold up a train. Found guilty after a lengthy trial, he was temporarily housed in the county jail in order that the court reporter could write up his testimony from which his court-appointed attorneys hoped to base an appeal from the verdict.

Two days later, on the night of September 28, 1891, three days before he was to be sentenced to San Quentin prison, he escaped from the jail. Although there are several versions of how he escaped, all the evidence points to efficient outside help.

Shortly after Grattan's escape, William Dalton was brought to trial on the Alila robbery charge and after ten days the case was submitted to the jury who speedily returned a verdict of "not guilty." Before the trial, Sheriff Kay predicted it would be impossible to convict a Dalton in that neighborhood. Before Bill Dalton left the courtroom he was arrested on a charge of complicity in a robbery committed in San Luis Obispo. Perhaps that arrest saved his life. At any rate, a year later it prevented him from accompanying his three brothers in the wild scheme of robbing two banks simultaneously in their own hometown of Coffeyville, Kansas. Within an hour, the gang's corpses lay piled in the street, a testament recording one of the greatest debacles in outlaw history.

38

III

Sontag and Evans:
Daredevil Robin Hoods
or Desperadoes?

"Evans and Sontag!" exclaimed Sheriff Jay Scott, as he pounded his fist on the table at a gathering of his posse. "What else matters but beating them? We must trample them to ground, or else they will become legendary!"

There is little doubt of the extent to which law enforcement and railroad personnel were obsessed with these two personalities during five years of chase. Their exploits were world news and avidly followed by the often hero-worshiping public from 1889 to 1894. Whether portrayed as Robin Hoods, victims of malicious persecutors, or as the most cruel, cold-blooded, and daring desperadoes ever to set dynamite to a treasure chest, the fact remains that their story was a tremendous melodrama. Indeed, these "Adventurers of the San Joaquin" were so extraordinarily ingenious that they would blow up and loot express cars, killing whoever stood in their way, and then unabashedly return to their small ranches and resume the quiet life of tilling the soil.

On a foggy night in late February, 1889, two masked men with heavy bags slung over their shoulders jumped aboard the tender of the Los Angeles bound Southern Pacific passenger train No. 17 as it pulled out of Pixley, a small

The Pixley station

settlement in Tulare County in the heart of California's San Joaquin Valley. One man was short and stocky, big shouldered with solid, weather-beaten hands. The other was taller and thinner and appeared to be a much younger man.

Without comment, the two scrambled over the dusty wood and jumped into the cab. The fireman fell back in terror as the two men appeared from nowhere. But because of the rumble of the accelerating train, engineer Piet Bolenger didn't hear them at first as he stared ahead into the dense tule fog. Suddenly, a Colt .45 jammed him in the ribs.

"Just stay loose, Engineer. You won't be shot if you do as you're told. Down the track a bit, you'll stop at a road."

The engineer smiled weakly and grunted an acknowledgment as he saw they were carrying shotguns. A few seconds later, one of the bandits shouted for the engineer to halt and the big locomotive groaned to a stop.

Compelling them to dismount, the bandits marched the

two to the express car. One of the bandits banged on the locked door with the butt of his shotgun.

"We ain't messing around. Throw up the strong boxes or we kill the engineer and fireman. Then we'll blow you to hell."

J. R. Kelly, the express messenger of Wells Fargo, quickly doused his lantern, jerked his shotgun off the wall rack, and screamed, "You can kiss my ass!"

One of the bandits laughed and immediately pulled a large demolition bomb from the bag looped over his shoulder. Placing it under the sliding doorhandle of the car, he screamed, "Git back from the door or you'll be killed!" and lit the short fuse.

In the meantime, curious passengers aboard the train began to wonder why the train had stopped in the middle of nowhere. Conductor Jackson Symington quickly made his way from the passenger cars back to the smoker where sheriff's deputy Ed Bentley from Modesto was on his way to San Diego for a vacation.

"This is unusual. It might be a holdup. You might give me a hand."

The deputy took his Colt from the pocket of his jacket hanging overhead and followed the conductor. Brakeman Henry Grabert joined them, picking up several lanterns on the way. As they neared the express car, a tremendous explosion rocked the train, almost lifting it from the tracks. Nearly the entire front of the coach was ripped open. As one of the bandits ran forward to climb in, he saw the brakeman's lantern and several figures running toward him through the fog. The masked man fired a barrage from his shotgun. Grabert fell forward dead, buckshot having punctured his entire body. A second blast tore away the deputy sheriff's left arm. He staggered back fainting from shock. Not wounded, conductor Symington turned and raced northward at full speed where the Pixley station was located a mile and a half away.

In the mail coach, express messenger Kelly was badly shaken by the explosion. As he tried to stand up, one of the bandits walked past him searching for the gold chests. Finding only one, the bandit cursed, but quickly lugged it through the debris and dropped it down to his waiting partner who had two horses ready. They emptied the gold coins and paper currency into their shoulder bags and rode away into the fog with the stunned crew watching in amazement.

Because most of the valley's farmers were enemies of the railroad as a result of numerous land lawsuits, mild celebrations broke out the next morning when word filtered down of the spectacular robbery. It wasn't that the two robbers had successfully gotten away with $5,000 as much as it was open defiance of one of the world's great railroads. Most of the farmers had eagerly joined the Settlers' Land League which took the Southern Pacific Company to court over the tenure and prices of lands granted to the railway by Congress to aid in the construction of the railroad through the fertile San Joaquin Valley. That controversy eventually led to the tragic Mussel Slough incident in which five farmers and two sheriff's deputies were killed during a mass meeting of the Land League. That massacre was remembered vividly for the next few years and the bitterness of the memory brought the farmers to cheer when they learned train No. 17 had been attacked.

The death of the brakeman was regrettable, of course, but how better could a man die than in an incident humiliating and costly to the railroad? Almost to a man the valley citizens regarded the Southern Pacific Company as a ruthless monster which destroyed all in its path. And there was justification for their hatred. During the early 1870s while the company was building its line through the valley, it enticed hundreds of farmers and their families to settle in the "agricultural wonderland." Southern Pacific hoped to establish a profitable freight and passenger business.

Sontag and Evans

Pioneers poured onto the sparsely settled railroad-owned land offered rent free. Immediately, they went to work reclaiming large tracts of arid land through complex irrigation systems.

After years of blood and sweat, this lowland section of California was quickly becoming the center of California's choicest wheat crops, vineyards, and cattle ranches. With their homes built and towns laid out, the farmers suddenly learned that the Southern Pacific was willing to "sell" them the land they had developed for over a decade for $30 an acre.

The settlers formed the Land League and scraped up enough of their hard earned monies to fight the case in court. But with state legislators and judges in the pay of Southern Pacific, the farmers lost. Fifty-two thousand signatures were then gathered by the Land League and sent to President Hayes for aid against the monopoly. But that too failed. In the meantime, the Southern Pacific raised the farmers' high freight rates. Tensions were high during a meeting at Mussel Slough. And when a sheriff and three deputies arrived, all hell broke loose. For this, 21 ranchers were convicted, even though a deputy provoked the gunfight.

At the end of the trial, the settlers knew they were beaten—all except Chris Evans who was determined to fight to the end.

Born in Vermont in May of 1847, Chris Evans was of typical New England rural stock. His family moved near Toronto in the early 1850s, although it soon became evident that the small Canadian farm could not support the entire family. In 1869, Chris and one of his younger brothers decided to head west in search of gold. Unable to find it in the Nevada and California mines, they settled down in the San Joaquin Valley as simple farm laborers. Evans soon married and built up a quarter section of land which he soon lost through faulty title. Deeply bitter, he

43

Chris Evans as a young man

moved to Tulare where he again settled and took up farming and served as a part-time agent for the California Bank in charge of warehouses in Tulare, Pixley, and Goshen. With these hard-earned monies, he moved to Modesto where he opened a livery stable in order to do grading for the Southern Pacific Railroad which was laying track down the valley. But within six weeks, a tragic fire destroyed his newly bought stable and horses and he was again broke. Evans took his wife and seven children to Visalia and again tried his hand at farming on 20 acres of land owned by his wife's relatives.

Though he had very little education, he was considered an intelligent, hardworking, and honest farmer. Stockily built, he was a strong man. His most notable features were exceptionally large ears and mouth, and a long, flowing beard. Although he was ordinarily reticent, he was known to have flashes of violent temper. But he was a typical farmer of the period and his neighbors liked and respected him. Indeed, he served on juries in the towns and counties in which he resided. Evans was thoroughly familiar with the territory and often thought of running for public office.

One hot Sunday afternoon in July, while refreshing himself after Church with a cold beer in a saloon as his wife Molly and children chatted and played with friends in the street, he overheard two strangers next to him discussing the injustices perpetuated by the Southern Pacific Railroad Company.

"The Goddam Southern Pacific will roast in Hell!"

Evans laughed and turned to the dapper little man with regular features and said, "Stranger, I couldn't agree more with you!"

The man smiled and introduced himself as George Sontag and his brother John. He explained that John had once worked as a brakeman for the Southern Pacific in Fresno. John then spoke up and explained how his foot had been caught between two cars and his right ankle crushed.

Evans shook hands with the brothers and ordered more beers as the three headed for a table to spend the afternoon. Learning that they had grown up in the same poverty and had suffered the hardships he had, an immediate bond was established.

John and George Constant were born in Minnesota in the early 1860s. After their father died, their mother married a man named Sontag and the brothers took the name of their stepfather. The boys headed west for Fresno in 1878 where they found work with the railroad. John vowed he would seek vengeance on the railroad because after his terrible accident, Southern Pacific had placed him in its' Sacramento hospital where his treatment was callous and indifferent. One day, he simply hobbled out, a bitter enemy of the railroad.

Evans soon discovered that John Sontag was an emotional, unpredictable man, quick to temper, and would

45

seek revenge for any slight, real or fancied. Though obviously intelligent, Evans did not consider him to possess his own native shrewdness, which in his thinking entitled him to be leader. Lithe and handsome, Sontag possessed an enthusiastic hatred for the Southern Pacific which Evans could put to good use.

On the other hand, George was a little fellow, goodlooking and the dressy sort. He impressed Evans as a clever talker. He had a trace of iron gray hair giving him a touch of distinction. But now, by his own admission, he was a confirmed criminal and perjurer. Instinctively, Evans did not like him as much. Later that evening, he told his wife that the man was "a bad actor, a man who doesn't possess the hardy qualities of his brother, the cheapest kind of bandit who has it in him to turn traitor."

A year passed after the Pixley holdup without arrests or clues turning up. No further attacks were made on the Southern Pacific.

The Goshen station

46

Then at 4:00 a.m. on January 24, 1890, two masked men again climbed the tender of train No. 19 as it left the small settlement of Goshen. In a carbon copy of the Pixley robbery, the engineer DePue and his fireman, Lovejoy, were marched to the express car where they were used as a shield by the bandits when demand was made on the messenger to open the door. Remembering the tragic consequences of resistance the previous year, the express messenger opened the door and threw down a sack of valuables. But unfortunately for an old tramp who had been riding on the brakebeams, one of the bandits shot him down in cold blood when the old man got off thinking the train had come into a station. Again the robbers were successful in escaping and eluding the posses. This time the bandits got away with $20,000. Investigations by railroad detectives and sheriff's deputies revealed that the same two men were responsible for both robberies. They also concluded the two would kill anyone suspected of getting in their way.

The San Joaquin Valley settled into its ordinary calm routine of labor, when on September 3, 1891 train No. 19 was held up again by the same two men in Goshen. This time they climbed on board as the train stopped in Modesto to let passengers off. The bandits then covered engineer Neff with their pistols ordering the train stopped and in the usual manner commanded the engineer and fireman to precede them to the express car. In order to prevent interference by the passengers, they fired several shots along the sides of the train. Their shots alerted the two express-messengers inside the mail-express car who prepared to fight.

When the robbers' command to open the door was ignored, they placed a bomb against the door, quickly exploded it and ordered the fireman to enter the express compartment through the shattered opening. The determined messengers shouted they would kill anyone entering the car and for the fireman and engineer to remain outside. Without comment Evans and Sontag quickly lit another bomb and tossed it into the car. After a few seconds, it was apparent the bomb was a dud.

In the meantime, two detectives of the Southern Pacific happened to be passengers on the train. Len Harris and J. Lawson hurried forward. Spotting the robbery in progress, they fired without warning. Surprised, Evans and Sontag stumbled back. Now, the two messengers opened a withering barrage of fire and the two bandits had no choice but to flee without securing the loot. In the next few minutes a running gunfight ensued and detective Harris was seriously wounded.

By this time, the feelings of the farmers were turning against the bandits. Although sympathetic with anyone attacking the railroad, they did not condone murder regardless of the victims. In this atmosphere, Sontag persuaded Evans to return with him to his old home in Minnesota where George was living.

On November 5, 1891, a train was held up at Western Union Junction near Chicago by three masked bandits who escaped with $4,800. Although the robbery was never solved, George Sontag admitted before his death that he, John, and Chris committed the crime. He stated that if John had not been in such a hurry to get away since he didn't know the environment, they could easily have gotten away with $100,000 and headed for South America.

But the three decided to head back toward California. Evans missed his family and figured the law still had no clue as to the identities of the bandits.

On their way west, the three spontaneously attempted to hold up a train near the Kasota Junction, Nebraska. Although they were unsuccessful and law enforcement officials could not directly connect them to the robbery, George confessed before he died that it indeed was the three of them who made the attempt.

Returning to Visalia in 1892, Evans decided that George

A Southern Pacific 80,000-pound wood-burner

would be a natural assistant in their future robberies and plans were made to rob train No. 17. at Collis in Fresno County. This was to be their most notable robbery and climaxed their reign of terror on Southern Pacific passengers up and down the valley.

At 11:15 p.m. on August 3, 1892, the method used in the Pixley and Goshen robberies was again repeated as the locomotive pulled out of Collis. The locomotive was rumbling along the tracks when three bandits suddenly appeared on top of the tender, faces masked and brandishing deadly shotguns.

"Pull this train to a halt!" one yelled.

Fireman Lewis dropped his shovel and poked engineer Phipps who nodded and slowed the train down. As the train crawled to a stop, the engineer leapt from his cab and disappeared into some nearby bushes. The fireman was about to follow when one of the bandits shoved the muzzle of his shotgun into his back, "You better come with us!"

Pushing the fireman in front of them, the masked men hurried back to the express car, firing their shotguns off to the side to intimidate the passengers. Without demanding or negotiating with the messenger inside the express car to open the door, one of the bandits quickly tied two small bundles of dynamite onto the sills of the two doors of the express car and lit the fuse. The force of the explosion did little damage and the cursing bandit then ran to the other side and tied another dynamite bomb under the car door. This time the explosion demolished the whole front of the car and severely wounded messenger Roberts with a dislocated shoulder and concussion. One of the bandits leaped through the smoking debris and aimed his shotgun at the nearly unconscious messenger sprawled in a corner.

"Please," the man begged, "don't kill me. I'm hurt bad . . ."

The bandit picked up the man's weapons and flung them out of the car. Grabbing the keys from the messenger's belt, he quickly removed three heavy canvas bags containing $15,000 in bills and coins. Within one of the bags, there were over $2,000 in useless Peruvian coins. While fireman Lewis was forced to carry this plunder from the car to the nearby horses, one of the bandits quickly placed a demolition bomb on the left piston rod of the engine. The three bandits then scrambled toward their loaded horses and a few moments later the sound of hoofbeats faded into the darkness.

Early the next morning, posses which had searched for the bandits on the previous occasions were again organized and pressed into action. This time, however, they were augmented with twelve men selected from the railroad detective force who were instructed to find the bandits at all cost—even if it was to be their lifelong assignmen⸀

The following afternoon, Chris Evans appeared on the main street of Visalia for the first time in months. To friends, he explained his considerable absence as having been in the mountains. A few hours later, George Sontag appeared explaining that he had just returned from the east.

But Evans and Sontag had been under suspicion for quite awhile. Detectives learned in their investigations that the two men had been loud in their denunciation of the railroad and what little descriptions the train crews could provide matched perfectly with those of the two men. At first, Southern Pacific detective Will Smith suspected the two of at least having knowledge of the bandits. Then he learned of Evans' subsequent departure for Minnesota and sudden reappearance the day after the robbery. When he discovered that John Sontag had hired a team of horses on the day of the robbery (supposedly to take a small vacation in the Sierras) and that neither he, George, nor Evans had been seen in Visalia that previous day or night, he was convinced he had his bandits. Not only that, but Smith felt he was within easy grasp of the $25,000 reward money.

Alerted that Evans and Sontag were in a popular saloon on main street, Smith and sheriff's deputy Ed Witty casually sauntered in. Smith walked up to Sontag after Evans left and began questioning him. Listening to his vague and contradictory answers, Smith asked Sontag if he wouldn't mind repeating his story over at the sheriff's office. Sontag obliged and, strange as it may seem, recounted an entirely different version of his whereabouts during the preceding afternoon and evening. He was promptly clamped in jail and held for further questioning.

Smith and Witty hopped into a buggy and drove out to Evan's home at the edge of town. As they approached the place, they noticed an unsuspecting John Sontag enter the ranch house from the barn. Rifles loaded and leveled, the two hitched the horses and buggy and walked up the steps. Without bothering to knock, they walked through the front door, startling Evan's oldest daughter, Eva, who was ironing in the living room. Sontag was often at the Evan's house, having become sweet on the pretty seventeen-year-old blond who had a figure which excited most of the young men in the area.

We're here to see Sontag. Where is he?" demanded Smith, leveling his rifle at the kitchen door.

"Mr. Sontag is not here," said the young woman, unaware that John had entered the kitchen.

"You're a goddammed little liar!" Smith snapped.

At that moment, Evans walked in to see what the commotion was all about.

"Where's Sontag?" Smith repeated, now pointing his rifle at Evans. Before Evans could respond, Sontag burst through the kitchen door blasting away with his double-barreled shotgun. Both Smith and Witty went down, blood and parts of their flesh splattering the walls. Eva began to scream as the two men groaned in agony.

"All right. Let's move on out of here!" Evans said. While Evans spoke to his daughter, Sontag unhitched the sheriff's wagon. Since the exchange of shots alerted the entire town, the two had to get away immediately. Indeed, as the two rode out the yard, they noticed various sheriff's deputies running down the road toward the house.

In a few minutes the Evans ranch house was surrounded by officers who found no one there but Eva caring for the' two wounded men. Witty had a severe shoulder wound with parts of his arm blown off. Smith had been peppered with several dozen shotgun slugs. After a search of the house yielding the masks of the bandits and after removing the two wounded officers to town, the remaining officers quickly organized a hunt, scouring the nearby lowlands and foothills.

In the meantime, Sontag and Evans were hurrying away as fast as they could without any food, blankets, or extra ammunition.

"They'll more than likely suspect we're heading for the Sierra timber," Evans told Sontag. "Well, let's just fool 'em!"

A few miles from his ranch, Evans pulled up alongside the road, jumped out, and cut the fence. After Sontag drove the buggy through, Evans quickly repaired it. The two then emerged and quietly made their way back to Evan's ranch in order to get their horses and stock up on supplies. But when the posse returned to Visalia late that afternoon exhausted from searching the delta of the Xaweah and St. John Rivers, Deputy Sheriff Dan Overall insisted that a small party of picked men surround Evan's home just in case they returned home for their loot, or for food and ammunition.

Six officers arrived at the ranch around midnight. But only a few minutes before, the two bandits had entered the corral. While Sontag was in the barn harnessing the horses, Evans sneaked up to a window and tapped on it until his wife answered.

"Any lawmen been around in the last few hours?" he inquired.

"No! But you're crazy to come back here! The whole town is talking about you two as the robbers," Molly exclaimed.

"I know. But we need food and ammunition."

At that moment, the small posse quietly arrived to encircle the house and barn. It was a clear moonlit night. Deputy Sheriff Oscar Beaver, who happened to be nearest the barn, heard activity within. Without hesitation, he shoved open the door and demanded,

"Drop what you're doing and get out here!"

He fired two shots into the pitch-black interior, hitting a horse. Sontag returned the fire, killing Beaver instantly. Now, all the other officers had the barn in a crossfire, rapidly firing buckshot every few seconds. But in the excitement, Sontag crawled out and toward the ranch house

Chris Evans' barn on the outskirts of Visalia

in between firing flashes. Within a few minutes Sontag linked up with Evans and the two escaped on foot, hiking over 12 miles through fields and back roads before they stole a team of horses and cart and proceeded into the Sierras.

When the news spread the next morning that the five deputies had declined to rush the barn but had waited for sunrise, the Southern Pacific detective force was in an uproar. It was said that A. S. Towne, general director of the Southern Pacific swore like a drunken sailor that the posse could be so stupid to let the bandits get away. Most of the residents were anxious to bring this chapter of California history to a close and over a 100 men volunteered to join the pursuit.

Evans and Sontag were indicted for train robbery and declared fugitives from justice. Three posses under the direction of Sheriff E. W. Kay of Tulare County, Sheriff John Hensley of Fresno County, and Southern Pacific detectives, were on their way by noon with high hopes of capturing their quarry by dinnertime.

E. W. Kay

But 48 fruitless hours later, the three posses straggled in empty-handed. Sheriff Day remarked, "They're both foxy customers. They know the trails like the backs of their hands. This ain't gonna be a picnic."

On October 27, George Sontag went on trial in the superior court at Fresno. Defense counsel Arnold Biggs attempted to delay the trial, pleading with Judge Holmes that Chris Evans and John Sontag were required as important witnesses. But the judge denied his motion and the case went to trial. A few weeks later, George Sontag was found guilty of complicity in the Collis train robbery and sent to Folsom Prison to serve a life sentence. The sheriff's officers were glad to get rid of him. They were under a constant dread that his friends might rescue him or that the jail would be blown up. Also, the cost of keeping him incarcerated in the county jail, plus the expense of additional guards was more than $10 a day.

During this time, a Wells Fargo search party uncovered four bags of gold coins in the yard next to Evan's ranch house. One of these bags contained the stolen Peruvian coins. However, the greatest break came when a friend of rancher Harvey Ward confided to Deputy Sheriff Witty that Ward had loaned the two escaping men a couple of mules and a rig. It seems that in their getaway, Evans and Sontag had managed to get as far as Ward's ranch. Ward knew that Evans had a mining claim near Sampson's Flat and obligingly loaned them what they needed. The friend insisted to Witty that Ward had not heard about the shooting since he was so far out in the swamps and was simply helping a friend. Actually, Ward later boasted that he would again aid anyone who could cause Southern Pacific such woe.

The bandits had used the mules to head northeast into the Sierra timber. When the road became so rough, the animals were abandoned and Evans and Sontag sweated the winding, twisting grade laden with provisions and ammunition supplied by Ward. But with every passing step, the fugitives were getting deeper and deeper into the rocky wilderness where they were leaving no trail.

The informant told Witty that Ward believed the two bandits were now hiding out at Evan's claim at Sampson's Flat. Witty didn't hesitate. Twelve deputies were quickly organized into a posse and headed for the claim. They were led by V. C. Wilson of Tucson, a former Texas ranger after the reward monies. From Arizona, he brought with him two Apache Indian trailers. In the party were Deputy Sheriff Andy McGinnis of Modesto, Constable Warren Hill of Sanger, and detectives Will Smith and Frank Burke. As the posse neared Sampson's Flat, they stumbled upon a small mountain cabin belonging to Jim Young who shared it with Ed Mainwarring. They could smell frying bacon, eggs, and potatoes. According to an eyewitness account by Will Smith:

It was 10 o'clock in the morning and we were hungry. Sight of smoke rising from Ed's cabin drew us forward, not

Sampson's Flat

Jim Young's cabin

knowing that our quarries were already quartered in the cabin and were even now watching us approach.

We started to go to Ed's house to get some potatoes. Wilson, McGinnis, myself, and Witty dismounted and strayed down the hill toward the house on the South side. I started off to one side toward a watermelon patch and Witty was with me a little bit to the rear. Wilson and McGinnis led off.

Suddenly, when the men were about five steps from the house, we saw two men run out and shoot. Wilson and McGinnis fell dead, but Wilson was reaching for his revolver and fell with it in his hands. Evans stepped over Wilson's body and started toward us, firing. He shot at Witty and one buckshot struck him in the neck. I fired at Evans and he then began firing at me with his Winchester. I ran to a pine log about 15 yards away and Evans fired at me three times. I got a good shot at him and when I fired

Reenactment at Jim Young's cabin while body
still lies in the yard

he dropped his gun and fell. One of the Indians said Sontag ran around the house and there met Evans. The two then disappeared.

Bloodstains were found on corn blades in the back of the place through which the outlaws took flight. From this it was assumed they had been wounded.

Rear of Jim Young's cabin

What had happened was that Eva had gotten word to her father earlier that Wilson, the confident ex-deputy from Arizona, was in town with his two Apaches to track him down. Also, she planned to send much-needed provisions to Ed's cabin in the next few days. The two bandits had abandoned Sampson's Flat to pick up the provisions before heading back to Minnesota.

When word reached nearby settlements that Sontag and Evans had barely escaped into the tall timber with little or no provisions, the mountains were suddenly alive with amateur and professional manhunters after the Southern Pacific and Wells Fargo reward of $25,000. Indeed, the rush to the mountain vastness was so great that a number of hunters abandoned the search in fear of being shot at by both pursuer and pursued.

During the following few days, the outlaws moved through the mountains the best way they could. Although both Sontag and Evans had suffered flesh wounds, they shrugged them off as insignificant. Without horses, provisions, or extra clothing, they were nonetheless glad to be alive.

On the second night of their escape, they knocked on the door of the cabin of Emil Tratten in Squaw Valley. Although Tratten knew Evans well, Mrs. Tratten was horrified.

"Please don't be scared, ma'am," Evans implored. "We're not going to hurt anyone except the railroaders who've hurt all of us. We'd just like a little something to eat and we'll be on our way."

Emil nodded to his wife who quickly prepared a chicken stew while Evans played with the Tratten's five-year-old daughter. Sontag stationed himself at a window, rifle poised.

"I sure wish I were home now with my own," he said, almost to himself.

After dinner, Tratten allowed them to sleep in his barn. The bandits were truly grateful and after a sound night's sleep were gone before sunup the next morning.

For the next ten months, the outlaws moved through the mountains asking, sometimes forcing, settlers to aid them. Although lawmen were receiving tips by the dozen, Southern Pacific officials angrily complained that local people were in league with the outlaws. Evans had scores of friends for miles around the region, where he had been a hunter, fisherman, and prospector off and on. Not only were lumberjacks and woodsmen keeping and feeding them, but it was hard to coax townsmen into search parties, even though the railroad would have paid handsomely for their efforts. Indeed, some people who still bore grudges against the Southern Pacific were openly cheering the bandits, although the majority of honest citizens were looking forward to the day when the tragic story would be over. On top of all this, people in the valley and the mountains now had a vast respect for the Evans-Sontag marksmanship. The point was clearly driven home that the pair was playing for keeps, dead or alive.

Winter was approaching and the mountains were due for their first snows. The hunt lagged more and more as rumors thinned. But the sheriffs, their deputies, and railroad detectives were under increasing fire. Ridiculing their efforts to track down the bandits, a newspaper humorist wrote in the San Francisco *Chronicle,* November 17, 1892:

> There is a rumor that Evans and Sontag have crossed the continent and are somewhere in Europe. It may well be that they have decided to spend the winter on the Italian Riviera. It would be easy enough for them to escape any time they want to since there is nothing to hinder them.

But if the hideouts of the bandits were a mystery to the detectives, it was no secret to Eva and Molly Evans. Chris was in almost weekly communication with his family through a friend who carried notes to Visalia and returned with greetings, gossip, and deployment of law enforcement personnel. Indeed, Eva later confessed the outlaws had made eight successful sorties from their mountain retreats to mingle with the family. And each time they came away with fresh supplies, clothing, and ammunition. Sheriff Kay, constantly being ridiculed, became very bitter. Both he and Southern Pacific general manager Towne openly declared there probably wasn't an honest man in the whole valley.

And to add fuel to the fire, a lumberjack rode into Visalia in early December, walked into the sheriff's office and declared he had a message from Evans.

"Well?" asked Kay, getting up from his desk.

"He told me to say him and Sontag are comfortable for the winter and are getting ready to come out this spring.

They had a nice Thanksgiving supper, roast quail and broiled trout!"

Beside himself with anger and frustration, Kay screamed as he threw the lumberjack out.

On Christmas Eve, Evans and Sontag quietly crawled into the Evans home. So happy was Sontag to see Eva that he announced to the family they were now engaged. They enjoyed a wonderful Christmas and New Years Eve and then returned to the hills again in early January.

With the coming of spring, the search was resumed in full force. But it wasn't until May 26 that the two robbers were again heard from.

S. J. Black of San Diego, one of the manhunters, was ambushed by the bandits in a small cabin he was occupying near Camp Bodgers. Although he was shot through the thigh, he was not badly wounded and that attack was to have important consequences.

When word reached Visalia of this attempted murder, U.S. Marshal Gard organized a posse of 14 deputies and railroad detectives. Will Smith and his men were howling for blood since Southern Pacific was losing passenger revenue because of possible new raids by the bandits.

With his men more determined than ever, Gard set out at 3:30 a.m. on May 28 with a posse including sharpshooters Hiram Rapelje, Fred Jackson, and Tom Burns. And for the next several days, they scoured the heavy mountain brush, becoming so exhausted they decided to rest for a day in an abandoned mountain shack.

Late that afternoon while cooking their evening meal, one of the posse spotted two heavily armed men casually walking down the path toward them.

"My Gawd! Here they are!" he exclaimed.

The posse ducked and crawled to their arms and took cover wherever they could. Sontag, who had always walked with a slight limp because of his earlier accident, was recognized beyond question as he approached the cabin. Evans was studying the cabin as he listened to Sontag who was absorbed in conversation. Suddenly, Chris Evans noticed something and hesitated, Sontag stopped and looked up. Will Smith, anxious not to miss a golden opportunity, panicked when he saw the two men stop and lift their rifles. Although over 100 yards from the waiting posse, Smith started firing. Immediately a barrage of bullets cut down the path. Chris Evans screamed and hit the dirt, his left arm nearly torn off by the heavy fusillade. Sontag fell behind a low mound of cow manure, watching Evans quickly crawl over between the bullets kicking up the manure like chaff. Evans began returning the fire with his good arm. As Sontag raised his rifle to fire, a bullet grazed his spine, nearly paralyzing him. Evans was firing with all he had.

In the meantime, Jackson and Rapelje scrambled out the backdoor of the shack and crept through the weeds to fire from the flank. Again near-perfect shots peppered the small pile of manure. Although the sun was now descending, Evans' fire shattered Jackson's ankle.

"We're getting out," Evans grunted.

"They've hit me bad," Sontag moaned, beginning to spit up blood. "I'm almost dead. Go on and I'll cover you."

"You're O.K. We'll make it together, or I'm not leaving," he said, as a second bullet ripped through his other good arm. With 14 men laying down such a heavy barrage, death was imminent. Returning an occasional shot, Evans and Sontag knew they were finished. When another bullet pierced Evan's right eye, flooding his face with blood, he whispered, "All right. That's it. I hate to leave you, friend, but there is no other way. If you make it, I'll get you out of jail."

Sontag begged Evans to shoot him, but Chris refused. It was now almost dark as Evans crawled off. Rapelje caught a glimpse of him and fired. But he missed. Bleeding from two wounded arms and half-blown out eye, Evans entered the timber and accomplished one of the most amazing feats of endurance ever recorded. He scrambled, climbed, and walked over sixteen miles through the cold night over some of the most inaccessible terrain in the Sierras to Wilcox Canyon where Mrs. Lige Parsons had a cabin. Stumbling onto the porch and collapsing, Mrs. Parsons put him to bed after tending to his wounds.

In the meantime, Sontag had taken a few more bullets. Nonetheless, he weakly fired back at the posse every half hour or so throughout the night. Members of the posse had such a high respect for him that they decided to wait until daylight before charging him. Camping around him the posse was able to get some sleep, content they were about to wipe out at least 50 percent of the notorious gang.

When the first morning light appeared, the 14-man posse cautiously surrounded Sontag and found him barely

John Sontag shortly after his death

alive, although subconscious. Thrown on the back of a buckboard, he died on the rough ride into Visalia.

The next morning, Mrs. Parsons further dressed Evans' wounds and gave him some coffee.

"I'm sending my boy for a doctor," she insisted.

"No you ain't" Evans protested. "All I need is a few more hours to rest, and I'll go."

"You are so badly hurt that unless a doctor sees to you, you'll be dead by sundown. Now, I'm sending for a doctor."

Realizing that further argument was useless, Evans calmed down and said "There's a lot of money for me dead or alive. If you split the reward with Molly, I'll do as you say."

The woman nodded her head in acknowledgment and later that afternoon Evans allowed himself to be arrested by undersheriff William Hall. He was incarcerated in the County jail in Visalia. His left arm was so shattered that doctors decided to amputate immediately.

During the weeks that followed, with Evans having been transferred to a jail in Fresno, theatrical promoters from San Francisco approached Eva and Molly with an offer to play leading roles in a melodrama entitled "The Collis Train Robbery." When the play opened at the National Theater on Jones and Eddy Streets in San Francisco, the theatre was filled to capacity. People from all over the Bay Area flocked to see the family of the notorious outlaw. The play continued for a number of weeks and when its sensation began to lose appeal, the company toured the main cities of the San Joaquin, including Visalia and Fresno, and headed for Los Angeles. Sontag and the Evans family were depicted as heroic figures while the detectives were seen as cowardly lackeys of the Southern Pacific. All $1700 the women earned was brought back to Fresno to hire the best available defense.

Evans' trial opened in Fresno on November 20, 1893, before Judge M. Harris. Chris was charged with the murder of Victor Wilson and Andrew McGinnis, the deputies

Chris Evans after his capture

killed at Jim Young's cabin. The courtroom was jammed with family, friends, and curious spectators and the newspapers assigned special writers to cover the case. The Associated Press wired a daily article to all its members on the progress of the trial.

The activities of the outlaws were so well known that it took nine days alone to exhaust four panels before a jury could be selected. The actual trial took fifteen days and the prosecution surprised everyone by announcing George Sontag as a witness, even though he had just made an unsuccessful attempt to escape from Folsom the week before.*

Sick and broken, and probably with the hope of winning a parole, George admitted that he and John and Evans had a hand in the Collis holdup, but he insisted that Pixley and Goshen robberies were the work of John and Chris alone. Still on crutches, he gave the impression of being a debonair desperado as he testified about the part each played in the robbery. At the conclusion of his testimony, the defense subjected him to a most severe cross-examination which showed him to be an ex-convict, a perjurer and a traitor to his brother. This took a great deal of weight from his testimony.

After the prosecution and defense rested their cases, the jury was locked up at 5:00 p.m. on the afternoon of December 13, 1893, until 10:00 a.m. the following morning. The foreman announced the jury had reached a verdict and that verdict was one of "guilty of murder in the first degree, with recommendation of life imprisonment." The prosecution's strategy had been to try Evans for murder and not for train robbery. This strategy had won, although law enforcement officials were disgusted at the recommendation of life imprisonment.

Shortly after the trial Evans apparently resigned himself to spending the remainder of his life in prison. Because he appeared so inwardly at peace with himself, Sheriff Kay allowed him to leave his cell and take his meals in a large cell tank. Gradually, he was coming to the best of terms

---

*Sontag had been hard at work on a rock pile near the American River when one of the inmates suddenly jumped the lieutenant of the guard, securing his rifle. With George as ringleader, seven men using the lieutenant as a shield, attempted to break through the circle of other rifle-wielding officers. But the lieutenant quickly jumped to the bottom of a slope, giving the officers the opportunity to fire at will at the inmates. Hiding behind rock piles, a small battle took place for a few minutes. When it was all over, three convicts were dead and Sontag severely wounded.

with his jailers. Actually, Evans was masterminding a clever escape.

During the closing days of the trial, Eva took her meals at the Acme Cafe in Fresno, where a young waiter immediately took a fancy to her. Believing that Chris Evans was the most heroic figure of modern times, he was ready to follow any guidance the beautiful blonde daughter might offer.

"Would you be willing to help Dad?" she inquired.

"Of course I would. No one has hated the Southern Pacific as much as me and your father."

"Well, you're the one who carries his food tray to him three times a day, aren't you?"

The next evening when waiter Ed Morrell brought Evans' supper into the jail covered with a napkin, jailer Ben Scott unlocked the cell door. Evans reached under the napkin, whisked out the .45 and leveled it at the jailer. Morrell then produced his own gun and Scott was disarmed and led out into the street where Morrell had a team and wagon waiting a few doors down in front of the Adventist Church.

As the three stepped from the jail, Sy Cole, a former mayor of Fresno bumped them. Evans shoved his .45 into the man's side and made him join the procession. As Morrell ran ahead to untie the team of spirited horses left near the church, he noticed J. D. Morgan, chief of police of Fresno, chatting with Bill Wyatt. Morrell walked up to the two men and ordered them to raise their hands. After grabbing the chief's gun and turning to search Wyatt, Morgan jumped Morrell. But Evans was on the scene and shot Morgan, who fell to his knees. Morrell and Evans then backed away toward the horses and carriage. But the tie-rope was slackened and the horses frightened by the shots broke from Morrell's grasp and sped away.

With the alarm given and commotion coming from shops and homes on the street, Evans and Morrell ran into

Ed Morrell

an alley, stole a tethered horse and wagon on the next street and galloped out of Fresno.

During that winter, Evans and Morrell remained in the Sierra foothills, traveling over the same trails Evans had the previous year with John Sontag. Once again the wanted men received food and shelter from the residents scattered throughout the region.

On January 11, two masked gunmen held up the Southern Pacific station at Fowler, managing to steal the pocket money of the agent and a few weary travelers. The next morning, Jim Hutchinson who had known Evans in Visalia met the two bandits on a lonely road north of Fowler and had a nice talk with him. Evans confided that he wasn't doing much dodging any more, although he enjoyed his freedom.

But what really infuriated lawmen was during the following week when Petey Bigelow, a reporter for the San Francisco *Examiner,* rode into the mountains near Sampsom's Flat and interviewed Evans—a story that made three columns on the *Examiner's* front page. Indeed, publicity was so widespread that Eva and Molly returned to San Francisco to once again appear before admiring audiences in *The Collis Train Robbery.*

Several deputies came upon Evans and Morrell near Badger early in February but were driven off by the outlaws' near-accurate bullets. When Sheriff Kay and Scott discovered that Evans and Morrell had dared to spend several nights in Visalia's Arlington Hotel, they were in a fury. The owner came in for an intensive grilling, although he swore he never recognized either man.

With Eva and Molly acting in San Francisco, and knowing of Chris' love for his family, Sheriff Kay decided on a trick that just might work. He spread the rumor that Tessie, Evan's youngest daughter, was near death with diphtheria. A Visalia physician gave substance to the rumor by making several trips to the Evan's home and telling townspeople she wouldn't last the week. Evans learned of his daughter's "illness" and without hesitation left his mountain hideout for his home. Morrell insisted on going along. Had Eva been around, she doubtless would have tipped her father off about the fake. Late that night, Evans and Morrell slipped into the house. Delighted to be with his children again and thrilled that Tessie was not seriously ill, Evans did not even bother to consider he was in a trap.

An hour later, there was a knock on the door. Evans swung it open and was face to face with 12-year-old Walter Beason, the neighbor's boy, who bashfully handed him a note:

Chris Evans: You are surrounded. Surrender and we will
protect you. If not, we will take you anyway.

E. W. Kay, Sheriff

Evans smiled.

"Well, I guess that's it. We're not having a shootout with
the kids here."

Chris then sent little Joe Evans, his 9-year-old son out to
find the sheriff and hand him a note reading:

Sheriff Kay: come to the house without guns and you will
not be harmed. I want to talk to you.

Chris Evans

Kay and Deputy Sheriff Will Hall approached the porch
without weapons and Evans walked through the door and
shook hands with Kay. Morrell grasped Hall's hand.

"Chris, we'll have to go now. This story is finally over,"
Kay said calmly.

"Yeah. And it's just as well. I'm ready." Evans answered.

A member of the posse brought up a wagon and the
prisoners were placed on it. The manhunt was indeed
over.

No time was lost in passing sentence. The time had been
set for 2:00 p.m. the next day, but the court moved the
hour up to 10:00 a.m. In the tense situation, the spectators
laughed when the judge called Evans "Christopher Col-
umbus" instead of "Christopher Evans." But Evans was
sentenced to life at Folsom, although through his counsel
he begged the court to make it San Quentin on account of
George Sontag being at Folsom.

Morrell was tried in the superior court of Fresno County
for the theft of Benny Cochran's horse and cart on the
night of the escape. At that time, horse stealing carried a
greater penalty than assisting in a jail break. Within 10

71

minutes of the verdict, he was sentenced to life imprisonment at Folsom. In 1896, he was transferred to San Quentin and remained there until March of 1908 when his sentence was commuted by the governor of California and he was released.

After serving 17 years, George Sontag was given a pardon for turning state's evidence in March 1908, the same week Morrell was released. For some time the two attracted attention by appearing together on lecture platforms speaking on "The Folly of a Life of Crime." But the two men didn't get along and Morrell disassociated himself from Sontag. Evans had written him a letter in which he characterized George as "Judas Iscariot" and the faithful Morrell quietly drifted into obscurity.

After serving 17 years under heavy security in the striped garb of a convict at the California State Prison at Folsom, Chris Evans was paroled on May 1, 1911. An old man, broken in spirit and health, it appeared he would not survive confinement much longer. Taking pity on him, Governor Hiram W. Johnson gave him his freedom. Unable to earn a living, he applied for admission to the county poor farm in Portland, Oregon, in January 1917. One of his sons read a newspaper account of his father's condition and had him removed to St. Vincent's Hospital where he died a week later.

The passing of Evans brought forth only a few short newspaper obituaries, most of which were brief reviews of his escapades in the San Joaquin, where once he had been known and respected as an honest hardworking business man and farmer, then later as train robber, murderer, and outlaw.

Evans and Sontag! Their story promises to remain the most notorious in the history of California.

IV

Browning and Brady

Night had spread its foggy mantle over the San Joaquin Valley. From Marysville to Bakersfield, the Valley was locked in with a cold gray gloom of near zero visibility. It was one of the first fogs of the winter, and John Kelly, the Southern Pacific trackwalker, pumping along on his small velocipede, was anxious to get home near Mikon, about three miles west of Sacramento. It was cold, icy cold, and in spite of his fur-lined jacket, Kelly found himself shivering as he coasted down the track.

Suddenly, he spotted a lamp on a large crate a few feet ahead of him and he cautiously stopped. No one was around and he felt an eerie sensation. At that moment, a big, broad-shouldered fellow in a soft cap stepped out of some bushes and approached him, a rifle slung over his shoulder. From the other side of the track appeared a slender, white-faced youth whose chin was buried in the depths of his coat collar and whose hands were thrust deep into his pockets.

"Howdy, men," Kelly said weakly as he forced himself to smile.

Neither man acknowledged the greeting and the sound of their footsteps on the crushed rock bedding sent a chill to the marrow of his spine.

73

"Git off!" the tall man finally demanded. With Kelly hesitating, the man unslung his rifle and Kelly jumped off. As he did so, the other man walked up to him and reached into Kelly's pockets and extracted a small purse containing five dollars. As he did this, the other bandit lifted the velocipede off the tracks and quickly smashed the wheels with the iron butt of his Winchester.

"We're going for a walk," the tall bandit announced as he returned. Forcing Kelly in front of them, they walked down the track about a quarter of a mile. The bandits were well armed, each carrying a Winchester rifle and cartridge belts, in addition to their revolvers. It was nearing 8:00 p.m. on that foggy night in October 1894 and the eastbound Overland Express was soon due to pass.

Kelly was handed the lantern and ordered to give stop signals to the engineer when the train approached.

About an hour later, the light of the express was seen cautiously coming down the track. Kelly signalled and engineer Scott brought the train to a stop. Climbing down from the cab, the engineer and fireman inquired what the problem was. At that moment, the two robbers appeared from the bushes with revolvers leveled against them.

Ordering Kelly, engineer Scott, and fireman Lincoln to precede them, the bandits walked toward the Wells Fargo express car. When the express messenger hesitated, one of the bandits shouted that the car would be dynamited and the three hostages shot on the spot. The messenger shoved the car door back and raised his hands.

Forcing the train crew to climb into the express car ahead of them, the bandits made a quick search of the car and found four sacks of gold and silver coins in one corner. Scott was then ordered to carry the sacks to the engine cab and the others were to remain in the car. The bandits then cut the engine and tender from the rest of the train and forced Scott to slowly move down the track for a few miles where the bandits jumped off and disappeared into the fog.

The grade near Mikon

The Southern Pacific and Wells Fargo Express Company officers, as well as Sacramento police, were notified of the holdup and although a vigorous search was immediately conducted, no trace of the bandits could be found. Scott, Kelly, and Lincoln described the robbers as rather tall, the shorter of the two being close to 5 feet, 9 inches tall. From their actions around the train, both men appeared to have a fair knowledge of railroading. They had been disguised in long, linen dusters and their faces concealed by legs of a pair of woolen drawers with holes cut in them for the eyes and mouth. Both had been cool and systematic during the robbery. The taller bandit had very slim, almost soft white hands. The shorter of the two had a thick Irish brogue. Law enforcement officials

75

quickly decided that the robbers were residents of Sacramento, or nearby settlements. It was believed the bandits buried their loot somewhere in the swampy ground on the Yolo side of the river.

A reward of $10,000 was offered by the Southern Pacific Company for the arrest of the robbers and recovery of the stolen $50,000.

Six months later, Southern Pacific passenger train No. 3 left Sacramento at midnight and headed east through the broad plain. With the locomotive gaining momentum, engineer Alvin Brown observed two men with bundles run along the track and climb aboard the head car. Since this was a common occurrence, he paid no further attention to the late arriving passengers. When the train arrived at the east end of the trestle over the American River a few minutes later, fireman Ralph Cole noticed the same two men now on top of the head car pulling on overcoats. Twenty minutes later, when the locomotive was only a few miles from Swanston, the shipping point for sheepmen, two hooded men walked over the coal tender and covered the engineer and fireman with revolvers.

"Stop the train," the tall masked man shouted and the engine crew slowly complied. The taller robber then asked the shorter man if that was the correct place and on receiving an affirmative answer demanded that unless the train was stopped immediately, the engineer and fireman would be killed instantly. When the train ground to a halt, the shorter bandit ordered the crew to climb down. As engineer Brown started to leave the cab, he quickly turned the "cut-out cock" below the brake valve, thus preventing the robbers from moving the locomotive.

The engineer was ordered off on one side and the fireman on the other side. Ordered to cut the train off at the express car, they could not accomplish it. The bandits then forced them to return to the engine and instructed them to proceed to the outskirts of Ben Ali, where they had cached a box of dynamite. Since Brown had turned the "cut-out cock," he could not start the train. He informed the bandits the brakes were stuck. The engineer persuaded the two robbers to return to the express car and learn what the trouble was. As they headed back, Brown turned out the lights in the engine cab, scrambled down the ladder, and hid in the tall grass nearby watching the action. When the robbers returned to the engine with the fireman, they held a short conference. Deciding the train could not be moved, they disappeared into the night without any plunder.

Although posses were immediately formed, no trace of the robbers could be found. But no one questioned who the bandits were. It was obvious by their method of operation that the two were the same men who robbed the overland express at Mikon.

The next appearance of the two daring bandits came six days later at the small station of Castle between Stockton and Lodi, California. The train selected for their next holdup was train No. 5 upon which there was a considerable shipment of gold. At this period in 1895, the ferry

Castle

"Soland" used between Port Costa and Benecia was in San Francisco for necessary repairs and it was necessary to detour all eastbound trains via Tracy and Stockton.

As the locomotive passed slowly over the Calaveras River bridge, a masked man leaped from the bridge onto the coal tender. From there he scrambled into the engine cab and demanded the train stop at Castle. As the train was stopped, a second hooded man waited while the engine crew climbed down and was marched to the express car. The engineer was ordered to call the express messenger to open the car. The messenger slid the door open just enough to fire two shots which missed the bandits, then slammed the door shut. The tall bandit threatened him with being blown up if he didn't get out immediately. The man waited a moment, then opened the door and jumped out.

The bandits forced the engine crew and messenger to get on board and then jumped aboard themselves. They made a quick search of the car and discovered the only money and valuables in the car were locked in the big safe. Because they didn't have sufficient dynamite to blow open the safe's door, they once again were unsuccessful in looting the train. However, one of the bandits confiscated the handsome revolver belonging to the express messenger.

As the bandits walked down the track, they fired some shots in the air to intimidate any passengers who might get some funny ideas about investigating the delay. Then, the two quickly uncoupled the engine and tender and departed in the direction of Lodi.

In the meantime, a westbound freight train arrived in Lodi, six miles east of Castle, with orders to stop and wait there until No. 5 passed. As it pulled into a siding, it observed the headlight of No. 5's engine moving very slowly toward Lodi.

As the train approached, conductor Jim Andrews on the freight saw that it was running light and that there was no one in the cab. As the engine passed, he quickly climbed aboard and brought it to a stop. Noticing the water in the boiler was very low and the engine in danger of blowing up, Andrews opened the injector valve, allowing water to enter the boiler. He then attached the engine from his freight and sent No. 5 to Lodi. While this was taking place, he sent a wire to the superintendent at the Oakland pier indicating there had been a holdup.

As the conductor climbed back into No. 5's cab to keep the engine hot and prevent further delay to the train, he found a stick of dynamite on the engineer's seat which he hadn't noticed before.

Sheriff Cunningham of San Joaquin County, detective Ahern of the Southern Pacific Company, and detective Snyder of Wells Fargo and Company arrived at the scene on a special train the next morning. That afternoon, chief detective Gard of the Southern Pacific Company, with detective Hume of Wells Fargo joined in the search. They discovered that the robbers had a horse and buggy near the scene of the holdup and trailed the vehicle to a county road where all trace was lost. But once again, the descriptions of the bandits tallied exactly with those who had robbed the trains at Mikon and Swanston and the method of operation was exactly the same. Since the two daring bandits had not obtained any loot in their last two attempts, it was expected they would strike again—and soon.

As the northbound train No. 16, the Oregon Express, was enroute to Portland through the fertile Sacramento Valley at 2:00 a.m. on March 30, two men were spotted boarding the blind baggage when the train stopped for a few moments at Wheatland. When the train resumed its journey and was about 10 miles south of Marysville, the two men put their hoods on and crawled over the tender down into the cab. With the usual procedure of covering the engineer and fireman with revolvers, the train was brought to a halt at an area known as Reed's Crossing. The engine crew was forced to climb down and walk with the robbers back to the express car where engineer Henry Bowser was ordered to tell the express messenger to open the door. Knowing that all the money and valuables were in a large safe, messenger Kelton opened the car door without hesitation. When the bandits entered and found nothing could be obtained without blowing the safe, they decided to enter the coaches and rob the passengers.

Ordering the engineer, fireman, and express messenger to precede them, they boarded the first day coach. The tallest outlaw quickly fashioned a bag from an old overalls leg and forced fireman Nethercott to accompany him into the car holding the bag. Threatening the surprised passengers with their Winchesters and having Nethercott pass the bag, the bandits secured close to $1,000 in gold, silver, and paper currency and 15 gold watches. Rewarded with such a large take, the bandits decided to rob the passengers in the Pullman cars.

But Sheriff John J. Bogard of Tehama County was a passenger in the first Pullman car. On previous occasions he had told brakeman Simmons that if an attempt was made to rob the train on which he was a passenger, he was to be notified so that he could capture the outlaws. Bogard had a reputation as a fearless officer. Now, with this in mind, brakeman Simmons whispered to a porter to alert the sheriff. Bogard arose, partially dressed himself, and hid behind one of the seats, preparing to kill the bandits when they entered the car. Accompanied by fireman Nethercott, the tallest robber casually walked through the car's forward door and sheriff Bogard immediately opened fire. His first shot hit the surprised robber over his heart, mortally wounding him. Believing that the fireman was the second bandit, he fired and wounded Nethercott in the neck and leg.

In the meantime, the shorter bandit had boarded the rear platform of the Pullman car behind the sheriff. Suddenly hearing the gun blasts, he rushed into the coach and shot the sheriff in the back, killing him instantly. Then, without paying attention to his companion's pleas for assistance or grabbing the bag of monies and gold watches, he jumped from the car and escaped into the darkness. Within a few minutes, the wounded bandit died.

While fireman Nethercott was quickly taken to the hospital at Marysville where his wounds were treated, railroad detectives from Sacramento rushed to the holdup scene. They discovered that the bandit who escaped had made his way to Marysville on a bicycle, one of two which had been hidden under a wagon bridge a half mile from the scene of the robbery.

Sam Browning and bride

The dead bandit was identified as Sam "Big Jim" Browning, who was also known as S. McGuire and Oscar Brown. Although he had a previous police record, he had been working as a farmhand in the upper Sacramento Valley for a short time. The description of the man who escaped was that of Henry Williams. But it was soon learned his

Sam Browning shortly after his death

true name was Jack Brady, a man with an extensive police record. The revolver found on the dead robber was identified as the gun stolen from the express messenger on train No. 5.

Though a complete search was made for Brady, he could not be found. It wasn't until July 26, 1895, that he was arrested posing as a hobo under a Sacramento bridge. He was quickly returned to Marysville and charged with murder in the first degree.

Preliminary hearing was held before Justice of the Peace Aldrick on September 2, 1895, at which time Brady entered a plea of not guilty. The hearing was concluded within two days and Brady was ordered held for trial in the superior court of Yuba County with a trial set for November 4.

The trial was held before Superior Judge E. A. Davis with the case bitterly contested. Defense attorneys W. H. Carlin and E. A. Forbes characterized the evidence as a "chain of rope and sand." In their closing arguments to

Jim Brady

the jury, they used considerable sarcasm in describing the activities of the officers and the prosecution witnesses. The case was presented to the jury on the afternoon of November 18.

On the following afternoon after deliberating over 25 hours, the jury returned a verdict of guilty of murder in the first degree and recommended that Brady be committed to the state prison for life. It turned out that one juror was all that kept him from receiving the death sentence.

On the day of his sentence, Brady requested he be sent to San Quentin since it was "healthier than Folsom." But the judge refused to grant this request, stating that in his case it was safer to incarcerate him at Folsom.

That very night Brady made a desperate attempt to escape. He quietly constructed a rope ladder and then proceeded to saw the bars of his cell. A half inch of bar was all that remained by daylight. However, that morning, he was delivered to the state prison at Folsom.

A footnote should be added to this chapter of two of California's most desperate criminals.

After the Mikon holdup, Browning and Brady stopped their locomotive at a point near the town of Washington which is surrounded by lowland and marshy country on the west bank of the Sacramento River. They dropped the sacks of coin to the side of the track and then carried them a short distance into the marsh. With the aid of their lanterns, they dug a shallow hole and buried their sacks.

However, a wandering hobo, known as "Karl the Tramp" (John P. Harmans) had picked out a spot in the brush nearby as his bedding place for the night. Hearing the noise of digging and muffled conversation, he watched the robbers and remained quiet until they left. After waiting a few minutes, Harmans dug up the sacks and realizing what he had found, he moved them further into the brush where he again buried them. Before doing so, he placed about $10,000 in his blanket roll and immediately headed for Sacramento.

"Karl the Tramp" now changed his entire mode of life. After a brief splurge in Sacramento, he moved to San Francisco and rented an apartment on Nob Hill. Dressing well and spending a great deal of money on liquor and women, Harmans quickly drew the attention of San Francisco police and it wasn't long before he was brought in for interrogation. Police officers believed the money had been obtained from some crime, but certainly did not connect him with the Mikon robbery since he did not fit the description.

But on the day of his scheduled arrest, Harmans left San Francisco for Sacramento, his $10,000 spent. Resuming his former life as a tramp, he was not heard from again until early in April 1896, when he was arrested. Upon being questioned, he disclosed the source of his sudden wealth. The grand jury of Sacramento County indicted Harmans on the charge of grand larceny because he took the money and converted it to his own use when he could easily have located its true owner.

His trial started on April 2, 1896, before Superior Judge
Hinkson of Sacramento County and continued until April
30 when a jury found Harmans guilty as charged. Since
Harmans made restitution of the portion of the money he
had not spent, almost $40,000, leniency was recom-
mended.

On June 1, 1896, Judge Hinkson sentenced Harmans to
serve three years at Folsom. Hinkson commented:

> I can readily understand that a poor man traveling
> through the brush and coming upon a large sum of money
> would be sorely tempted. There was nothing in the evi-
> dence to show that you were a criminal. Yet, you had ample
> opportunity to reflect and seek out the rightful owner of
> the property.

After serving a few years at Folsom, Harmans was released and once again resumed the life of a tramp.

Brady was released from Folsom on parole on December 2, 1913, after serving 19 years, and became a
rancher near Galt, California, where he died a few years
later.

V

The Suisun Bay Bandits

As engineer Jack Marsh sat in the cab of passenger train Number 10 as it pulled out of Benecia on the night of April 16, 1910, he gazed across at the beginning of the rich San Joaquin Delta from the Solano side of the Carquinez

Jack Marsh

Straits. It was warm and the full moon cast a bright glint on the oily, tawny waters. Although he was running twenty minutes late, the peaceful scene of cottonwood groves in the flat of the small valley and wide shining circle of the bay reassured him that he could make up the lost time by speeding between Benicia and Suisun.

He lighted his pipe and reached for the throttle. His fireman gave the bellrope a pull, and soon, with the locomotives connecting rods clanking and her 76-inch drivers banging over rattling switches, the train was racing through the still night. They were now passing through the government arsenal at Benicia.

As Marsh turned and reached for an oilcan on the shelf, he suddenly found himself staring into the muzzles of two automatic pistols. Two hooded men of nearly the same height were facing him and the equally surprised fireman. They had obviously boarded the tender at Benicia.

"Step down from the throttle. I'll run the engine," one of the bandits said as he walked over to the engineer, menacing him with the pistol. The other bandit ordered fireman Jim Blakely to keep up steam.

Jim Blakely

When the train reached a point about one mile west of Goodyear, five miles east of Benicia, in a low, flat, marshy country, one of the robbers who had been keeping a lookout ahead said, "That will do; stop here!" The other man applied the air brakes, bringing the train to a stop. As soon as the train had halted, the engine crew was asked the position of the express car. The engineer replied the train did not carry an express car since it was a mail train.

The masked men then took the engineer and fireman back to the door of the mail car and had the engineer call to the mail clerk to open the car. The mail clerk wouldn't obey, and put out the lights in the car. Then one bandit, who had reached the door on the other side of the car with the fireman, threatened to blow up the car. This threat was repeated by the other bandit. The door was then opened and sacks of second class mail thrown out. The two mail clerks were told to throw out registered matter and about fifteen sacks of this class of mail were thrown to the ground. The mail clerks and engineer were ordered to pack this mail to the engine cab, and while they were doing so, the fireman was forced to cut the engine from the rest of the train.

When the mail had been loaded on the engine, the bandits departed on the locomotive with one bandit acting as engineer. When they reached the Goodyear bridge, the engine was brought to a stop and a number of the mail sacks quickly carried down from the right-of-way and loaded into a boat. Then the engine was turned loose with the throttle opened. Advice of the holdup had been telegraphed ahead to Tolenas, and when the conductor of a freight train on a siding there noticed there was nobody in the locomotive cab, he opened a switch, heading the engine into the siding where it collided with two freight cars.

The robbery was immediately reported by the train crew to Southern Pacific officials at Oakland Pier as well as the sheriff's office of Solano and Contra Costa Counties. Search of the right-of-way was made and sacks of mail were

The Overland Limited near Goodyear

found lying alongside the track at Goodyear, Cygnus, and at Joyce. The latter two evidently fell from the engine while it was in motion. The sack found at Joyce was cut open but evidently none of the contents had been removed. A long black overcoat worn by one of the bandits was left in the cab of the engine.

The morning following the robbery, Southern Pacific officers searching the vicinity found 41 sticks of number two dynamite in the grass at points near the robbery scene. Shortly afterward a sawed-off shotgun with a belt containing twenty shotgun shells was found under a bridge crossing Goodyear Slough. As the shore of the bay could be reached quickly from this point, it was concluded the bandits walked over the marsh to the Carquinez Straits and made their escape in a boat.

Working on this theory, a thorough search was made of the Contra Costa shore. It was learned that two young men who had kept entirely to themselves took possession of a deserted cabin on what was known as the Frazier Ranch, on the outskirts of Martinez about the first of April. These men caused considerable comment among the neighbors since their only occupation seemed to be rowing about the Carquinez Straits in a skiff. This continued for about two weeks at which time they became slightly acquainted with a Mrs. Hoadley who lived on a ranch nearby. One of them cleaned up her yard in exchange for foodstuffs.

A farmer living near Bullshead Point discovered a skiff that had been used by the same two men. It was floating about forty feet off shore in some rocks. There were very plain marks showing where two men had scrambled up the bank. As the skiff was immediately recognized as having been used by the two men, a search was made of the cabin they had occupied. Under the floor, the officers found more dynamite, similar to that discovered at the scene of the robbery. Where the boat was floating they found a pair of rubber boots like those worn by the men occupying the cabin. Close by on the bank, was a Colt's Army model .38 caliber pistol.

When the boat was pulled ashore, two cards were found covering registered letters which had been mailed on train No. 10. A farmer informed the officers that the last time he had seen the young men around the boat was about 11:30 a.m. on the 16th when they climbed in the boat near his place. At this time one of them had a large package concealed by a long black overcoat similar to that found in the locomotive and the other carried the rubber boots.

The officers then learned that a horse and buggy belonging to Mr. J. Hoadley had been stolen on the night of the robbery. A description of the horse and buggy was broadcast by telegraph and telephone to all officers in the bay district.

Checking in Martinez, railroad detectives learned that one of the bandits had left a watch to be repaired at a local jewelry store. On the same day the robbers inquired about the purchase of dynamite at the McNamara Store. The clerk explained to the two men that the dynamite was stored at the McNamara warehouse. Investigation at the warehouse disclosed that the greater portion of a box of dynamite had been stolen.

Southern Pacific's chief special agent Kindelon checked with the manufacturers of the shotgun found at the bridge, and learned it had been sold to the Riverside Cycle and Arms Company in Riverside, California. Following up with this company it was discovered that the shotgun, and four Colt revolvers were a portion of the loot secured in a recent burglary. The numbers of the stolen guns were obtained and furnished to all officers on the Pacific Coast.

The Southern Pacific Company offered a reward of $5,000 for information leading to the arrest and conviction of the robbers, and circulars containing this information along with the best available descriptions of the robbers were widely distributed.

Although numerous other clues were followed up, none led to the arrest of the bandits. It was learned that the watch left in Martinez had also been stolen from the store at Riverside, as well as a pair of field glasses, which were found on the bank near where the boat was floating. Further search of the cabin disclosed several shirts and underwear bearing a laundry mark "825" and others bearing the laundry mark "D-33." Efforts to trace these laundry marks were made all over the United States.

On July 15, Constable Michael Judge of Sacramento arrested two men driving a horse and small wagon. He believed the buggy to have been stolen. The specific charge upon which they were arrested was theft of a bale of hay. After the prisoners had been taken to the city jail, a search was made of their wagon. To Judge's surprise, three revolvers were found in the wagon and their numbers matched the guns stolen from the Riverside store. Judge called Southern Pacific police officer Eicke to verify the list. Eicke immediately notified Kindelon of the arrest.

The men gave their names as Joseph C. Brown and Charles B. Dunbar and denied participating in the train robbery. They were taken to Fairfield and questioned further by the district attorney and sheriff of Solano

County as well as by railroad police. After a thorough grilling in which both denied any guilt, it was decided to rest them for a day or so until various witnesses could be brought to confront them.

However, on the evening of July 19, Brown was brought into the sheriff's office at Fairfield and questioned by district attorney Raines, Sheriff McDonald and assistant chief special agent Harrold of the Southern Pacific Company. After being informed that witnesses were ready to identify him as one of the bandits, he broke down and made a complete confession, implicating his partner Dunbar.

Following Brown's confession, Dunbar was questioned, but still maintained his innocence. He was then informed that Brown had confessed and portions of the confession were read to him. But again he refused to admit any complicity in the train robbery.

In his confession, Brown admitted the burglary of the Riverside Cycle and Arms Company, and also stated that after the train holdup they drove to Riverside County in the stolen rig, rented pasture for the horse and remained in that vicinity for some time. They then stole a horse and wagon and burglarized the post office at Armada in Riverside County in June of 1910. In the post office burglary they obtained a small amount of stamps, $20 of the postmaster's personal funds, a shotgun and a pair of field glasses.

On July 22, both men were brought before Justice of the Peace W. W. Reeves for preliminary examination on the train robbery charge, and each took the witness stand and made full confessions covering the train holdup. As a result of this hearing they were bound over to the superior court, and held in the Solano County Jail.

On August 22, Dunbar and Brown were tried before Superior Judge Buckles at Fairfield. Each entered a plea of guilty to the charge of train robbery and Dunbar was sentenced to serve 45 years in the California State Prison at San Quentin and Brown to serve 45 years in the California State Prison at Folsom.

Brown escaped from a Prison road camp on May 11th, 1917, and was never apprehended. Dunbar was paroled December 24th, 1919.

In conversations with Kindelon, Brown and Dunbar admitted these were not their true names since both came from very high class families. Brown stated that his father had a very good government position in Texas and was prominent there. Dunbar, whose true name was believed to be Bishop, claimed to be the scion of a prominent Connecticut family.

These men were prosecuted by Joseph M. Raines, who was at that time district attorney of Solano County and who was known as one of the most able prosecutors in California. When the men entered pleas of guilty, Raines informed the court that by reason of the pleas they had saved the state considerable time and expense and requested the Court to take this into consideration with fixing the sentence. Judge Buckles said he would make allowance for this action by Brown and Dunbar and that it had been his intention to sentence each to 50 years, but in view of what Raines had stated would reduce sentence to 45 years.

VI

Jean LaBanta

"My husband is a crook!"

With these words, an attractive, well-dressed young woman confirmed the suspicions of E. L. Warner, baggageman for the Southern Pacific Company at the San Francisco Ferry Building. A few days before Warner had been asked by San Francisco detectives to be on the lookout for certain baggage believed to belong to a man known

E. L. Warner

as Clyde Kaufman, who was wanted on a forgery warrant by the sheriff of Placer County. This baggage was found to be on hand at the Ferry Building and three days prior to denouncing her husband, the young blonde had attempted to gain possession of it without the duplicate baggage checks. She informed Warner she had lost the checks, but could identify the baggage.

Having the detectives' warning in mind, Warner took the matter up with the general baggage agent and was instructed not to deliver anything without duplicate checks. Warner explained this to the woman who identified herself as Mrs. Dowling. It was suggested she take the matter up with the general baggage agent. As soon as she left the baggage room, Warner telephoned chief special agent Kindelon of the Southern Pacific Company describing what had happened. Kindelon in turn notified San Francisco detectives John Conlon and Walter MacKay.

But when she returned a few days later, she calmly told Warner that her husband was a crook and that he had left her for another woman. Warner then learned where her husband was living with the other woman. After she left

Mrs. Jean LaBanta, alias Mrs. Dowling

95

the baggage room, Warner again notified the officers. The man's address was a San Francisco hotel in the tenderloin district. Later that day, January 20th, 1914, Conlon and MacKay arrested Jean LaBanta, alias Clyde Kaufman on the forgery warrant for the sheriff of Placer County.

When Sheriff McAuley was notified, he hastened to San Francisco and returned LaBanta to Auburn to stand trial for passing a $65 worthless check. When the officers checked up on LaBanta's forgeries, it was found they totalled over $40,000. But, enroute to Auburn, LaBanta remarked to the sheriff he was not afraid of the forgery charge and dropped several hints that he was involved in "much more classier crimes." McAuley interrogated LaBanta closely. The evasive nature of his replies caused the sheriff to place an informer with him in the Placer County Jail cell.

About two weeks after they had been in the cell together, LaBanta confessed to the informer that in addition to his forgeries, he was responsible for the robbery of mail cars on Southern Pacific train No. 23, on October 14th, 1913; train No. 77, on November 17th, 1913; and train No. 9, on January 10th, 1914.

Train No. 23 had made an exchange of mail in Burlingame, California, and was slowly leaving the station when mail clerks Pete Scott and Bruce Titus were startled to observe a masked, armed man enter through the side door of the car. Menacing the clerks with his revolver, the bandit ordered them to lie down in the forward end of the car and pull mail sacks over their heads.

The train stopped at South San Francisco and although baggageman Mike Dempsy threw a sack of mail in the open door of the car, he did not notice the clerks. The robber threw out a pouch which was empty. After the train left, the clerks heard the robber searching the car. But they could not tell where or exactly when LaBanta jumped

Burlingame station

from the car. However, a passenger riding in the smoker saw a masked man leap from the train as it slowed down at Mariposa Street crossing in San Francisco while the train was moving six miles an hour.

In the meantime, the clerks did not remove the mail sacks from their heads until the train had stopped at the Third Street Station where they immediately reported the robbery. The only description they could give of the robber was that he was well dressed, about 32 years old, five feet ten or eleven inches tall, weighing about 180 lbs, and had a fashionable green fedora hat.

Although post office inspectors and Southern Pacific detectives made a thorough search for the bandit, he had made a clean getaway. LaBanta's first attempt at mail train robbery was a complete success, although the loot obtained was no more than $100.

His second appearance as a mail train robber was on November 17, 1913. Observed around the train while it was in the yards at San Jose, he was not suspected since he was dressed in overalls and jumper, the typical dress of a railroad man. He courageously grabbed hold of the mail crane on the mail car of train No. 77 as it was leaving San Jose enroute to San Francisco and he swung into the open door of the car.

97

After LaBanta held up the mail clerks in the same fashion as on his previous attempt and secured what appeared to be valuables, he stood at the doorway of the car. When the train slowed down near Burlingame, he jumped.

When detectives were notified, they knew he was the same man who held up the clerks on train No. 23. A search was made of the train's right-of-way in an effort to pick up the bandits' trail. Near the point where he jumped, the overalls and jumper he had worn were found.

Every effort was made to trace these clues and all merchants in the area were questioned. Though numerous persons were investigated, the search was fruitless. Again, the bandit had made an escape without leaving a worthwhile clue to his identity. Because the amount of plunder was again small, it was expected the bandit would soon attempt another train robbery in the area. Southern Pacific decided to have armed officers ride all passenger trains operating between San Francisco and San Jose. Somehow, LaBanta discovered this move and decided to head for southern California.

Jean Dolley, alias Jean Deslys

But before attempting his third train robbery, LaBanta took into partnership a young man of many aliases who had been released from San Quentin a few months before. Jean Dolley, alias Jean Deslys, alias Jimmy Barry, had just completed a sentence of 18 months for forgery. To LaBanta, he was known as Jimmy Barry and it was under this alias that he was known to officers.

Train No. 9 was scheduled to leave Los Angeles for San Francisco at 10:15 p.m. on January 10, 1914. About two minutes before the train was to depart, a well dressed masked man heavily armed entered the mail car through the open door where the incoming mail had just been delivered. Mail clerks A. G. Wendland and D. W. Perry didn't notice him enter.

A. G. Wendland

"Hey!" LaBanta shouted. "Throw up your hands. Put empty mail sacks over your heads!"

When they complied, a second robber who had been on watch outside the open door jumped aboard the car and closed the door behind him. A hurried but systematic

D. W. Perry

search took place. Clerk Wendland was asked the location of the sacks containing the registered mail. Wendland confessed where a number of registered sacks were piled, but did not mention that more valuable registered matter was concealed in a corner of the car. Wtih their backs to the wall, the clerks heard the bandits slashing the registered mail sacks and rifling the contents. When the train had reached the crossing at Tropico which lay between Los Angeles and Burbank, about fifteen minutes had passed. The air test was made and the train slowed down. At that moment, the clerks heard the door open and the bandits jump.

Though the clerks only saw the one bandit, there were sufficient clues to indicate who one of the robbers was. As a result of the painstaking investigation made on the slender clues and some further information obtained by the officers from other sources, Barry was arrested a few days after the robbery. He was indicted by the United States Grand Jury for the southern district of California on February 10, 1914, on the charge that he in company with another bandit assaulted mail clerks Wendland and Perry and took from them $600. On February 17, Barry entered a plea of not guilty but changed his mind on March 6 and pleaded guilty. He was sentenced to serve five years in San Quentin.

Though closely questioned by the officers, Barry denied taking any part in the two previous robberies in which the clerks were compelled to pull the mail sacks over their heads similar to this robbery. But he refused to identify the other bandit.

Every clue was painstakingly investigated, but officers could not learn the identity of the bandit leader. Barry refused to give any information and there was little direct evidence upon which the investigaiton might be based.

Sheriff McAuley

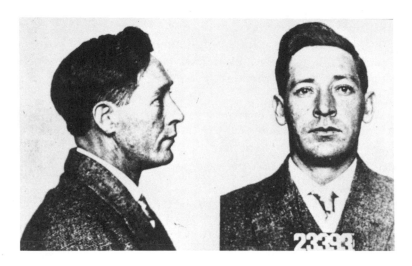

JEAN LA BANTA.

Aliases: Clyde Kaufman, R. Manning, J. C. Donnelly, R. Gordon, H. Gordon, F. C. Norris.

Description.—Age, about 35; height, 5 feet 10 inches; weight, 152; medium dark complexion; dark chestnut hair.

Bertillon.—77.7; 87.0; 92.5; 18.9; 15.1; 13.7; 6.0; 26.4; 12.3; 9.9; 50.0.

Sentenced February 11, 1914, San Francisco, Cal., to serve 25 years in State penitentiary, San Quentin, Cal., charged with the robbery of San Francisco, San Jose & Los Angeles R. P. O. train 23, October 14, 1913, between Burlingame and San Francisco, Cal.; and train 77, same R. P. O. November 17, 1913, between San Jose and San Francisco, Cal., and in effecting both robberies placing the lives of clerks in jeopardy by the use of a dangerous weapon.

Indictment returned at Los Angeles, Cal., February 10, 1914, for robbery of San Francisco, San Jose & Los Angeles R. P. O. train 9, at Los Angeles, Cal., January 10, 1914, pending.

Previous record.—Received at San Quentin, Cal., penitentiary, April 16, 1911, from San Benito County, Cal., to serve 2 years for grand larceny. It is also reported that La Banta is wanted in several counties in the State of California for passing fictitious checks. History 24817.

Jean LaBanta

Nothing of a positive nature was learned until LaBanta became boastful while riding with Sheriff McAuley, and the informer's information while in the same Auburn cell. After his confession, LaBanta was positively identified by the mail clerks on each of the trains as the robber. He also confessed to a large number of forgeries and on making a further check, the officers uncovered numerous forgeries he did not mention in his confession extending over a long period of time.

On discovering he had been trapped, LaBanta talked freely regarding his criminal career. He discussed his relationship with the woman, whose jealousy over his deserting her for another, resulted in his arrest.

As the train robberies carried a more severe penalty than forgery, it was decided that LaBanta be brought to San Francisco and tried in the United States Court on a charge of mail robbery. He appeared before United States District Judge Maurice T. Dooling on February 11, 1914 and entered a plea of guilty. After lecturing LaBanta, Dooling sentenced him to serve terms totaling 54 years in the California State Penitentiary at San Quentin. However, the sentences were set to run concurrently making a net term of 25 years. He was released on parole September 24, 1926, after having served twelve years.

Though possessed of a wide streak of vanity, LaBanta was intelligent and shrewd. He did not give the officers a great deal of information regarding his past life other than to detail the train robberies and forgeries. He always remained somewhat of an enigma.

VII

Anderson and Ryan

As train No. 25, "The Owl", was gathering speed on the night of February 17, 1915, after a stop at Saugus Station located at the southern entrance to a long arid stretch of flat country which is at the base of the Tehachapi Mountains, two bandits climbed aboard the engine. Leveling revolvers at engineer Walt Whyers and fireman Fred Harvey, the bandits ordered the train to stop two miles out of Saugus. Whyers complied and as the train was brought to a standstill the bandits ordered the engine crew to get off and uncouple the mail car. When this had been accomplished the engine crew was ordered to run the engine and mail car farther north.

When the car stopped the second time the bandits commanded the engine crew to accompany them to the door of the mail car. Firing once through the window to intimidate the mail clerks, the bandits commanded the fireman to call to the clerks to open the door. However, clerks Sherman Gebhart, A. Brown, V. Curti, and George Wearne hurriedly extinguished the lights in the car and piled mail sacks against the door. Then they sprawled on the floor at the rear of the car with their revolvers ready.

One of the bandits shouted, "Open that damn door or we will fill you full of lead." Unanswered, the bandits

The Southern Pacific "Owl"— observation platform

threatened to dynamite the car if the door was not opened. The mail clerks did not move. A volley of shots came through the windows and door and once more a threat of dynamiting was made. To this the mail clerks replied, "Look out, we are going to shoot!" This spirit of defiance and loyalty so completely unnerved the bandits that both turned and dashed into the open country where they were quickly swallowed up in the darkness.

The engineer and fireman returned to the engine and backed to the remainder of the train. Recoupled, the train proceeded no more than 30 minutes behind schedule.

During the time the passenger cars were idling at the point the train had been first halted, there was a great deal of fright and confusion among the passengers. Among them walked a soft-spoken, smiling, middle-aged man insisting there was no danger and to calm down. Though no

Train No. 25,

one knew his identity, this quiet, reassuring fellow was none other than William Sproule, president of the Southern Pacific Company, who was returning from a convention at Los Angeles. He succeeded admirably well, the passengers settling down to wait for help.

Southern Pacific detectives and sheriffs of both Los Angeles and Santa Barbara Counties were notified and they immediately formed posses to track the bandits down. However, they were not successful and the bandits made good their escape.

Two young hobos, William Miller and John Fuller, who had been loitering around Saugus on the afternoon of February 17, were arrested and questioned regarding the holdup. However, they furnished descriptions of two other men who had been in Saugus on that afternoon with whom they had pitched horseshoes. All four were waiting for a train on which they intended stealing a ride. They

"The Owl"

stated that when "The Owl" was leaving Saugus, they attempted to board the head end with the other two men, but were ordered at the point of pistols to go to the rear if they wanted a ride. They claimed to have been on the roof of a Pullman car when the holdup took place, and observed the uncoupling of the mail car and locomotive from the rest of the train.

The descriptions furnished by Miller and Fuller tallied with those given by the engine crew and a determined search was made of all hobo camps and places.

On February 24, a week after the attempted robbery, two men giving the names of Edward Collins and Frank Ryan were arrested in Napa for the burglary of the post office at Rutherford, a small settlement near by. It was immediately noticed that these men answered the description given of the train bandits. Miller was brought to San Francisco and immediately identified Collins and Ryan as

Sherman Gebhart

William Sproule

Frank Ryan

being the men who had boarded the head end of the "The Owl" at Saugus and held up the engineer and fireman. Collins' true name turned out to be Nola Anderson.

In a search of the room occupied by Anderson and Ryan at Napa, officers found dynamite corresponding to that found on the doorsills of the mail car. Seventy dollars worth of stamps were also found.

Now that federal authorities had conclusive evidence that Anderson and Ryan had burglarized the post office, it was decided they would be tried on that charge, although there was no doubt they were the men who attempted robbing "The Owl." On March 13, 1915, both men entered pleas of guilty to the charge of burglarizing the post office at Rutherford before Federal Judge W. T. Van Fleet in San Francisco. Anderson was sentenced to serve three years and Ryan to serve eighteen months in the California State Penitentiary at San Quentin.

"What made you a bandit?" Van Fleet asked Ryan.

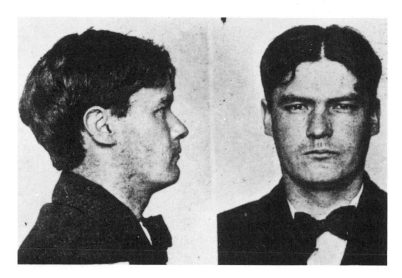

Nola Anderson

"Bad companions and dime novels." answered the Australian. "Jesse James was my favorite hero. I used to read about him at school when us kids swapped dime novels. We played wild west games out in the prairie when we ran away from school."

"And what made you a bandit?" the judge asked Anderson.

"Dime novels and bad companions," was the answer. "I had a lot of 5-and-10 cent novels and I liked to read them. But I always wanted to be the hero and not the villain, although some of them has the robber for the hero. I always liked the Old Sleuth books and the Jesse James books, too. But more important I wanted money. I hung around tough dumps and fellows there pulled off jobs that got big wads of money. That's the way it started."

The United States Immigration Department ordered the deportation of Ryan to Australia on May 29, 1916, when he was released from San Quentin. Anderson was discharged from San Quentin on July 4th, 1917.

VIII

Roy Gardner

When Roy Gardner's life is considered, one is impressed with his ability to perform miracles in escapes, for the simple reason he believed the old adage, "If you want a thing done well, do it yourself." In the escapades which made him a national figure, Gardner was outstanding proof that the man who believes he can do something, and is willing to risk, has a 75 percent chance of being successful even in the face of the mightiest odds.

Unlike other criminals who laughed at prison bars and manacles, Roy Gardner believed in taking unexpected risks. Unlike others who have successfully escaped from official captivity, Gardner did not count on outside aid. To his credit, it is true that he bore no hatred or malice toward his law enforcement personnel and never for a single second considered his freedom worth the life of a fellow man. Roy was content at making a "dash for freedom," and in his various attempts he never hurt anyone. Indeed, in his most dangerous train robberies, he placed a wooden bullet in his gun in order to ensure the safety of officers or clerks who might resist.

Aspiring to the title, "King of Escape Artists," Gardner achieved notoriety not only as a mail and train bandit, but as a master in the art of successfully escaping from the

111

Roy Gardner

grim walls of the United States Penitentiary at McNeil Island in Puget Sound.

Gardner was born in Trenton, Missouri, on January 5,
1886, of respectable parents. When he was eight years old,
his family moved to Colorado Springs, where his father
became interested in mining and later operated the elec-
tric light and power plant. Gardner attended the grammar
and high schools, graduating from the latter at 16. In his
school days, Roy demonstrated the quick thinking that
served him so well in later years.

After completing high school, Gardner drifted back to
Missouri, working for about a year; then he returned west,
continuing to Arizona where he worked in the mines. Not
enjoying the work, he decided to join the Army and enlisted in the Twenty-Second Infantry at Fort Worth,
Texas. This regiment was sent to the Phillipine Islands in

1903, remaining there about two years. Roy returned to San Francisco in February, 1906. But with only a few months more of his enlistment to serve, he deserted in March 1906, heading for New Mexico's mining properties. He remained there until 1908.

Then, he again decided to travel and went into Mexico at Nogales, wandering as far south as Culiacan and Mazatlan. Roy remained in Mexico about five months and returned to Arizona where he made connections with a gang engaged in smuggling ammunition to the Carranza Army which was attempting to gain control of the government from DeLaHuerta. Gardner had accumulated sufficient money from various jobs to purchase a team of mules and a wagon, and obtained backing to go in business as an ammunition smuggler. In March 1909, he was arrested at Cananea by the Mexican authorities while attempting to deliver a wagon load of ammunition.

Gardner was taken to Hermosillo where he was sentenced to death and thrown into an old dungeon. In that jail were three other Americans. Together they plotted escape. Gardner noticed that in the early morning hours, the sentry patrolled his beat in a listless, sleepy manner and he decided to cut the wood away from the lock on the ancient cell and break out, attacking and disarming the sentry. When the locks had been sufficiently cut and the prisoners completed preparations for the escape, Gardner volunteered to attack the guard. As the sentry wearily plodded past the cell, the prisoners forced the door and jumped him. Gardner clobbered him behind the ear, knocking him unconscious. The Americans quickly dragged the guard out of sight, bound and gagged him, and took possession of his rifle and ammunition. The three silently crept to where the sentry at the gate was dozing. He too was quickly overcome and his arms and cartridges confiscated. However, the prisoner who had secured the first sentry's rifle had secured the second guard's cartridges in the struggle. He now carried a

Springfield rifle with Mauser ammunition. The other pair fared no better, having a Mauser rifle with Springfield ammunition.

On leaving the prison they separated into pairs hoping to reach the American border. On the second day, Gardner and his partner discovered their mistake when they had used their last Springfield shell in killing a rabbit. They then decided to split up, each attempting to reach American soil on his own. After a long, torrid, and harrowing trip across the desert, and weak from hunger and thirst, Gardner succeeded in crossing the border at Naco, Arizona. This trip would have killed a weaker man, but Gardner's strong physique had saved him and he was soon in good health and spirits. He learned that his partner had also crossed the border, but the other pair were recaptured and executed on the spot.

Roy worked around the mines for six or seven weeks, until he had sufficient funds to travel to Trinidad, Colorado. Here he learned his family had moved to Oklahoma City. While at Trinidad, Gardner tried prizefighting, winning by a quick knockout. He then made his way to Oklahoma City and engaged in five fights, winning all. Returning to Trinidad he was matched with "Fireman" Jim Flynn, a ranking heavyweight, and Gardner was knocked out in the sixth round after a stirring fight. With this setback to a pugilistic career, he decided to come to San Francisco, where he was successful in securing a contract to do some blasting at Rockaway Beach. Making considerable profit on this contract, the money lasted while he led a life of idleness until December 1910.

During December he managed to secure a few dollars at odd jobs, but on Christmas Eve he found himself with only a dollar left. While walking down Market Street, the window display at the Glindemann Jewelry Store attracted his attention. After gazing at the display for a few minutes and turning over in his mind the possibilities of escaping with some of the precious stones, Gardner entered the store and asked the clerk to show him some diamonds. When a tray of the loose stones was placed before him, he snatched it up and raced from the store, turning the corner from Market Street into Ellis Street. Detective Sergeant George McLaughlin was walking on Ellis Street toward Market at a leisurely pace and when Gardner approached on the run, McLaughlin observed the tray in Gardner's hands. He turned in pursuit and shouted at a traffic officer on duty at Powell and Ellis. The officer intercepted Gardner and hurled him to the sidewalk. McLaughlin then placed handcuffs on him, while the traffic officer hurriedly picked up the diamonds which were rolling all over the street. Gardner was tried on a charge of robbery before Superior Judge Lawlor and sentenced to serve five years in San Quentin.

But because of his assistance to the captain of the guard during a riot in the prison's cafeteria in 1912 at which time Roy was seriously injured, he was paroled six months later. He then went to work at the Mare Island Navy Yard as an acetylene welder in January 1913. During this time he was working at Mare Island, Gardner met and wooed Dolly Nelson and was married in June. Shortly after his marriage, Roy quit and opened a welding shop in Oakland. This shop burned down a few years later and Gardner and his wife took a trip to Los Angeles on the steamer *Governor*. Enroute, the *Governor* collided with the *S.S. McCullough*, with the *McCullough* sinking. Mrs. Gardner took twelve photgraphs of the wreck which she loaned to the newspapers and to the government officials investigating the disaster. For this she received numerous letters of appreciation. On September 23, 1917, a daughter Jean was born to the Gardners.

Within a few weeks Roy was recommended to the Shaw-Batcher Shipyard in South San Francisco by the Linde Air Products Company as a superintendent of welding. He worked there until after the Armistice. During this time he was active as a speaker advocating the purchase of

Liberty Bonds. When resigning from the Shaw-Batcher Co., Gardner explained he was going to open a welding shop in Fresno with his brother-in-law. He believed the two of them could create a new industry in that part of the San Joaquin. This plant was opened in February 1919, but business did not develop in any great volume and Gardner sold out six months later. Moving to Los Angeles, he secured a contract to manufacture a number of large tanks for the Union Tank and Pipe Company, a contract he completed in four months,. making for himself and his little family a good profit. Early in April 1920, Gardner decided to take a vacation in Tijuana and since his wife was not interested in joining him, she headed for San Francisco with the baby to visit relatives.

Between drinking bouts and unlucky visits to the gambling tables, Gardner's savings dwindled to only a few dollars in a short time. On April 27, 1920, he walked up to the general delivery window of the San Diego post office to see if any letters had come in for him from Dolly. While waiting in line he observed a bank messenger deposit a package of currency with the clerk at the next window. Gardner's funds were very low and he didn't want to face Dolly with the news that he gambled away all their savings. Temptation was very strong to regain his losses. When Gardner heard the clerk mention that the package was bound for Los Angeles, he loitered around the post office, hoping to learn the movement of the Los Angeles mail. He discovered it was to be transported to the railroad station in trucks.

That night Gardner returned to the post office armed with a pistol. He lurked in the shadows until he noticed the trucks being loaded shortly after midnight. As a truck containing what appeared to be registered packages moved slowly into the dark alley away from the post office, Gardner jumped on the rear. When the truck had picked up speed, Gardner crawled over the mail sacks to the back of the driver's seat and thrust his gun into the driver's ribs.

Brusquely, he commanded him to pull over to the curb. As the truck halted, the driver was ordered to point out the registered packages. The surprised driver disclaimed any knowledge of registers on his truck until Gardner threatened to kill him. Pointing to several packages the driver stated those were all the registers he had. Gardner cut open several pouches, jamming the contents into his pockets. He then grabbed several small pouches and jumped from the truck, shouting for the driver to drive on.

Gardner hurried back to his room where he went over his plunder. To his dismay he found he had about $80,000 in securities and some Canadian currency. After hiding the money, Gardner went to a restaurant and had breakfast. He then rented another room where he slept until evening. After rising and having dinner, Roy purchased all the newspapers containing account of the holdup and returned to his second room for the night. He read the newspapers and then lapsed into an untroubled sleep, feeling secure he had not left any clues to his identity.

But during breakfast the following morning, other newspaper stories gave new details of the robbery and the mention of his name as a suspect in the crime made him almost throw up. He was now a suspect because of the several small mail sacks he had left in his first hotel room together with his suitcase which had his name stenciled on it.

Roy rented an automobile and went back to the second room where he gathered up his loot. He drove to Del Mar, a small town outside of San Diego, and walked out into a small field to bury the bonds and currency. He then walked along the railroad right of way to conceal his footprints. Returning to San Diego, he was immediately arrested because a young fellow had observed all his actions and notified the police of his burial and description. Faced with this identification, Gardner confessed and the loot was now back in the hands of the Railroad Express.

The driver of the mail truck identified Gardner as the bandit and he was also identified as the man who had rented the room in which the stolen mail pouches were found. Preliminary hearing was set for the following day, when Gardner entered a plea of guilty. Bail was set for $25,000. He was sentenced the following day to serve 25 years in the federal penitentiary at McNeil Island.

Gardner was brought to Los Angeles and held in the County Jail for several days. With a broken heart, Dolly arrived from San Francisco and was surprised to learn that he had once been an ex-convict at San Quentin. She said, "When you never told me how you spent those years in 1911 and 1912 I thought you had been married and wouldn't confess. I'm glad that you were in prison."

On June 5, 1920, along with two other federal prisoners, Gardner was placed on a train in Los Angeles. Deputy Marshals M. Cavanaugh and H. Haig were in charge of the small group headed for the state of Washington and McNeil Island Penitentiary. In Fresno, the train stopped to pick up two Chinese prisoners and proceeded north. When the group reached Sacramento, Gardner asked permission to telephone his wife in San Francisco for a few minutes. Since Roy had been a model prisoner on the journey, the marshals granted his request. Perhaps the most painful moment of his life occurred when Dolly lifted her daughter Jean to the phone to say a few words to her daddy. It was at that moment that Roy decided he would escape at all costs.

Again boarding the train, Gardner remained passive until the following afternoon after the train passed through Salem, Oregon. Looking out the window almost the entire route, Roy suddenly leaned forward in his seat and shouted, "Wow! Look at that ten point buck!" Haig leaned over to get a better look and Gardner grabbed the marshal's gun from its holster and swung it to cover both guards. Amazed and angry, the officers raised their hands. Before they could entirely recover, Gardner reached over

and took Cavanaugh's gun. He then ordered one of the
Chinese to take the keys from Cavanaugh and unlock the
handcuffs of all the prisoners. Gardner then ordered the
officers to be handcuffed together. The other two prisoners stated they didn't want to escape since they had a short
time to serve. But since the two Chinese sentenced to six
years each for narcotics smuggling had long terms ahead
of them, they decided to join him.

Gardner asked the marshalls how much money they had
on them. Cavanaugh claimed he was broke and Haig said
that all he had on him was pocket change. But one of the
Chinese pulled $200 from Cavanaugh's pocket. Gardner
ordered everyone to sit back and enjoy the scenery for a
while since Gardner had some thinking to do.

The train chugged on for several hours through the
beautiful Oregon mountains as the small party sat together. Although extremely tense, they greeted conductors and passengers who continually walked by. When the
train finally pulled into the Portland yards, Gardner bid
the marshals a friendly goodbye and opened a window in
the drawing room and jumped out. Followed by one of the
Chinese, he ran to the edge of the yards where he indicated he was now going to escape alone. Gardner then
raced back into the neighboring mountains where he
headed north. Walking all night, he eventually reached
Ranier, Washington. He promptly stole a motorboat and
cruised down the river to Astoria. From there, he purchased a first class ticket to Bellingham, traveling through
Tacoma and Seattle. In Bellingham, he stole an auto and
drove to Sumas on the Canadian border and crossed un-
observed into Canada. In Vancouver, B.C., he boarded
the Canadian Pacific and rode comfortably to Moose Jaw,
Saskatchewan, where he obtained a job as a welder. A few
months later, he crept back across the Canadian border
into Minneapolis. There he quickly succeeded in becoming a salesman of welding equipment because he knew the
trade so well. For the next several months, he traveled

throughout the midwest demonstrating and selling this equipment. After accumulating several hundred dollars in commissions, he resigned to become a welding instructor at the Davenport Auto School in Iowa. Remaining in Davenport for another several months where he developed a reputation as a fine teacher, he again promptly resigned and headed for California.

Along the way, he could not restrain himself from robbing several mail pouches from the express cars of midwestern railroads.

But Gardner eventually arrived back in Sacramento on May 8, 1921, and impulsively telephoned his wife who was working as a domestic in Napa. She quickly arranged to meet him that evening outside her home. But the switchboard operator had been instructed to warn the Napa sheriff if any strange phone calls came in for Dolly. She promptly notified the sheriff's office of the conversation she overheard. Gardner traveled to Napa and, although deputies were stationed around the house, managed to sneak through the line and see his wife for a few minutes. When the alarm was given, Gardner successfully eluded the officers and returned to Sacramento. From Sacramento, he headed north to Roseville, a railroad center about twenty miles away.

Gardner remained in Roseville for several weeks, keeping to himself and mingling with the public only when he went into a restaurant or watched the poker games in the nearby Porter House Hotel. People in Roseville thought he was living a simple life devoid of any drinking, gambling, or other bad habits. He presented himself as very frugal and thrifty.

On the night of May 19, train No. 10, an eastbound mail carrier, was robbed of two sacks of registered mail from a storage car in Sacramento. Although two men were seen by the engineer, it was at first thought Gardner was responsible even though he usually worked alone. Nonethe-

The Overland Limited

less, this robbery led to hundreds of circulars containing Roy's photograph and description being distributed throughout the district. And, of course, it led to a renewal of the intense search for Gardner, particularly when it was learned he had visited his wife.

On the night of May 20, as train No. 20 was leaving Roseville, railway mail clerk Ralph Decker who was sleeping in the storage car was rudely awakened by a man kicking him. As Decker stumbled to his feet, the man shouted, "Throw up your hands before I blow your head off!" Decker saw the man was armed and complied. He was then ordered to stand before the bandit who quickly tied his hands together using a leather strap he carried with him. The bandit demanded to know where the registered mail was and Decker stated he did not know if there were any registered pouches on the train. The masked robber

Ralph Decker

cut open several pouches and looked at the contents, throwing what appeared to be valuable into a small pile in the middle of the floor. During this time the robber kept Decker in front of him. Decker was then questioned as to whether the train stopped at Auburn and when Decker replied he did not know since this was his first run on the line, the bandit searched him, confiscating his mail keys, watch, and eleven dollars.

After robbing Decker, Gardner slid open the side door to gauge the speed of the train. Then, having accumulated a pile of registered mail, the robber took an empty mail sack and ordered Decker to hold his head the other way and open the sack. Into this sack was tossed the mail taken from the other pouches which filled the sack half way. He placed this near the open door. The robber gruffly requested Decker to tell him the stop signal and the mail clerk stated it was either two or three pulls. Reaching for the signal cord the robber gave it several pulls, but since the train did not lose speed, Gardner yanked both the signal and emergency air cords. The train slowed immediately because of the application of the emergency air. As the train was about to stop, Gardner kicked the sack of mail off and jumped from the left side door.

The train had reached the west end of the Newcastle yards at the time Roy jumped. After the train stopped, Decker notified the conductor who quickly sent a wire from Newcastle notifying the superintendent in Sacramento of the robbery. The Southern Pacific officers and post office inspectors were promptly advised. From the description furnished by Decker of the lone bandit, the officers immediately knew Roy Gardner had once again succeeded in robbing a fast moving passenger train.

Gardner's footprints were found leading toward the point where he had kicked off the sack of mail and by following the general direction of the prints, officers found the mail sack the following morning. It had been missed by the bandit in his hurried search in the darkness. With all the commotion in Newcastle, Gardner decided it would be unwise to continue searching for the pouch and disappeared into the rugged mountains.

Several photographs of Gardner were then shown around Roseville and other settlements. Mrs. Verdi Pitsos, wife of the proprietor of the Peerless Cafe, who served as a waitress recognized the photographs as that of a man known as Neal Gaynor who had been eating at the restaurant all through May. In fact, she had mentioned to Neal Gaynor how he resembled the photographs in the Sacramento papers of Roy Gardner and the man laughed and stated that Gardner had been captured a few days before.

Railroad and postal inspectors were detailed to watch the Peerless Cafe while the remainder of the various posses thoroughly searched the surrounding country. Clues poured in, although none turned out to be helpful. Finally, on May 23, the officers reported that they had observed Gaynor entering the cafe. This news was telephoned to the chief special agent in Sacramento. Accompanied by Agent McShane, post office inspectors Bill Austin and Jan MacCaulley, the posse rushed to Roseville by car. There, they were met by officer Al Locke, who informed them that Gaynor was in a gambling room at the Porter House Hotel.

Several officers were quickly detailed to guard the exits from the gambling room and chief special agent Dan O'Connell with the others entered the room in a casual manner. McShane remained close to the doorway while Austin and McCauley positioned themselves along two side walls of the room in an easy lounging manner. After observing the man known as Gaynor long enough to be sure he was Roy Gardner, O'Connell followed by Locke walked casually along the wall in order not to disturb the other card players, toward the table where Gardner was gambling with his back to the front door. The officers had entered the room so quietly that Gardner, though always cautious, was not aware they were present. As he reached to pick up the deck of cards to deal, the chief special agent drew his pistol and held it against Gardner's side, telling him to stand up. The others at the table were told not to be frightened because an arrest was being made. Gardner looked up and smiled, asking if he might have a few more moments to play out his hand since he held three queens. O'Connell smiled and nodded in approval, after Gardner was searched for a weapon. Gardner won the pot but invited the other players to split it since he was not going to be needing it for awhile. Then under close guard, he walked out and met the railroad inspectors who addressed him as "Roy." As the men stepped out into the street, Gardner was again searched by agent McShane who reached inside a slit in the side of his olive drab shirt and removed an automatic pistol. The gun was fully loaded and in a most accessible place. He could have pulled it out as the men were walking through the crowded cafe, but

Roy had chosen not to. He confessed that someone might get hurt.

Gardner was identified by mail clerk Decker as the man who robbed him and among Roy's possessions was found a leather strap similar to the one used in tying Decker up. A few days later a complaint was filed against him in Sacramento and he was ordered held on $25,000 bail.

Having been indicted by the United States grand jury in San Francisco, he was brought before U.S. Judge Joseph Van Fleet and entered a plea of guilty of robbing the U.S. mail. He was then sentenced to an additional 25 years. While waiting for his trip to McNeil, Gardner confessed that he stole the mail pouch in Centerville, Iowa, in March of 1921; the mail from the Southern Pacific Station in Bakersfield, California, in March of 1920; and various bags of mail at the station in Palisade, Nevada. After pleading guilty to these charges, he dictated his autobiography to a stenographer from the chief special agent's office. O'Connel sat in on Gardner's reminiscences and attempted to get Roy to confess also to the theft of the mail pouch from train No. 10 in Sacramento on May 19. Although Gardner denied participating in this robbery, he hinted in such a manner as to suggest that he indeed was the guilty party. A day later he informed Southern Pacific detectives that he heard a conversation between two men regarding the disposal of the loot obtained in that theft and he would lead them to the plunder if his wife Dolly would share in the insurance reward estimated to be $5,000. The agreement was acceptable to the officers. On June 9, Gardner was brought to the place he indicated. Under heavy guard, he pointed out an unusual tree and stated positively that the booty was buried there. But a thorough search failed to disclose any of the property. Indeed the officers could find no indication that the sacks had ever been there. A few days later, Roy admitted that this had been a hoax and that his intention was to escape if an opportunity presented itself.

Roy Gardner

That same night, he was placed on train No. 12 in the care of deputy U.S. Marshall Tom Mulhall and guard Alvin Wrinckle. Not only was he heavily manacled, but a tight-fitting 50 lb. "Oregon Boot" was placed on his foot so that he could not escape. In Dunsmuir, prisoner Norris Pyron was put on board also bound for McNeil Island Penitentiary. Southern Pacific officers rode the train to Portland in order to assist the government officers. Reaching Portland, a request was made to have the Southern Pacific detectives continue to Tacoma, a request which was quickly granted by the main San Francisco office.

The train left Portland at 11:00 p.m. and once again, Gardner's conduct and attitude was exemplary. He was apparently resigned to serving his sentence and remained quiet and subdued even though a 50-year term was facing him in one of the most isolated penitentiaries in the world.

After the train left Vancouver, Washington, at 1:15 a.m., the deputy marshals decided to retire and the Southern Pacific officers were told they could leave the drawing room in which they all rode. Gardner was in pain wearing the double chains and Oregon boot.

After the railroad detectives left the drawing room, the shades were drawn and the door locked. Gardner asked to use the toilet. Since he had not asked for some six or seven hours, his handcuffs were removed and he stepped into the toilet section of the drawing room. While there, he removed from a belt next to his skin a small .32 caliber revolver which he had managed to conceal on the various occasions he was searched. With this gun now in his hand, he stepped quickly from the toilet and ordered the stunned deputy marshal Mulhall to throw up his hands and stand up. Wrinckle was sound alseep on the coach seat. Stepping into the open portion of the drawing room he told Morris Pyron to step down from the upper berth and put Wrinckle's handcuffs on Mulhall and Wrinckle who was now awakened. Pyron also placed leg irons on the officers. Gardner walked up to Wrinckle and relieved him of his gun, ammunition, and spare cash. Mulhall had about $120 on him and Roy was delighted.

About 2:45 a.m., the train had to take on water at Castle Rock, Washington, and slowly pulled to a halt. When he felt the brakes being applied, Gardner put out the lights and raised the shade to look out. Since everything appeared to be in total darkness, Gardner decided this would be as fine a place to escape as any other. He quickly opened the window and allowed Pyron to jump first. Then removing the cartridges from the small .32 pistol, he tossed it to the officers, saying, "Fellows, you can keep this as a souvenir." As he was about to jump, he turned and returned to Mulhall and clasped the Oregon Boot on his foot, adding "I generally don't go in for cruelty, but you've got this coming to you."

Soon after the two fugitives left the train, the chained officers were able to unlock the drawing room door and summon assistance. The alarm was spread quickly and a search for the criminals was started by the local officers. This latest escape caused nationwide publicity to again be focused upon Gardner. His name was on every tongue and his crimes and daring escapes recounted in every newspaper in the United States.

On June 12, one of the posses located Pyron near Kelso, Washington. Pyron informed the officers that shortly after they left the train, he parted company with Gardner and had not seen him since. Pyron claimed that Gardner did not give him any of the money taken from the officers, which was undoubtedly true since Pyron had only a few pennies in his pockets.

Enlarged photographs of Gardner had been hurriedly prepared and sent by the chief special agent of the Southern Pacific to special agents of the various railroads in Oregon and Washington with the request that they be distributed around the smaller towns along their lines. On the morning of June 14, word was received that Gardner had visited a restaurant in Castle Rock, ordered breakfast, and when he noticed several people looking closely at him, he left the place hurriedly without finishing his meal. The posses returned to Castle Rock and made thorough searches of the entire vicinity, guarding all roads and attempting to close every avenue of escape from that territory.

For two days there was no let up in the intensive search. Then a telephone call was received from special agent McMurray of the Northern Pacific that Gardner was under arrest at Centralia, Washington. When questioned at the city hall in Centralia, Gardner admitted he had been in Castle Rock on the fourteenth and beat his way to Centralia on a freight train. At Centralia he registered at a hotel, using an alias and on the following day observed one

of the large photographs of himself on display in the railroad station. He also discovered the same photograph on
the front page of the local newspaper. Fearing recogni-
tion, he purchased a quantity of bandages and several articles of clothing and made his way to a lonely place where
he could change his clothes and bandage his face.

A dramatic touch was added when Gardner was entering a restaurant a few hours later and the patron called
out, "Here comes Roy Gardner now!" Although the re-
mark was said in fun, Gardner nearly lost his nerve and
walked out. But he smiled weakly and remarked, "If I
were Gardner, I'd collect the reward myself" and cooly sat
down at the counter ordering a huge meal. After casually
surveying the restaurant, he ate his meal and slowly sauntered out. Walking quickly down a side street, Gardner
registered at another hotel, using a different alias and decided to keep to his room as much as possible. Everyone in
the northwestern part of the United States was looking for
him.

But because of his numerous bandages, the landlady of
the second hotel became suspicious that her roomer was
suffering from some contagious disease and notified
officer Louis Sonny of the Centralia Police Department.
Dubious that the man might have a plague, Sonny casually
walked up to Roy's room and knocked on the door. When
Gardner answered, Sonny questioned him about his accident. Roy calmly explained that he had been injured in a
gasoline explosion in Tacoma. Sonny was not satisfied and
grew more and more suspicious. He decided to bring
Gardner to the city jail even though he himself was not
armed. During a brief exchange in the jail, Sonny was
joined by special agent McMurray of the Northern Pacific
Railroad who had been aiding in the search for Gardner
and who had distributed the photographs sent him by
O'Connell in San Francisco.

McMurray saw this man and hesitated. He immediately

asked Gardner to unravel the bandages. Roy protested, saying that this would cause him a good deal of embarrassment. No one was now laughing and Sonny immediately called the city physician who removed the bandages. As the last few bandages were removed, Gardner started chuckling.

That night Gardner was quickly removed to McNeil Island under heavy guard. Shackled to two officers until he was delivered to the warden at the U.S. penitentiary, officials would make sure he would never escape again.

When Gardner was received into the penitentiary and the heavy steel door slammed shut, the post office inspectors, U.S. marshals, and railroad detectives breathed a sigh of relief. There had never been a man like Roy Gardner before. He was finally in prison: a penitentiary from which no man had ever escaped before. A prison on an island surrounded by swift and treacherous currents, the water was nearly always icy cold. With sentences totaling fifty years before him it was felt that Gardner would spend the rest of his life in that grim dungeon.

On entering the routine of prison duties, Gardner's cheery attitude and ready acceptance of the usual prison rules soon allayed any suspicion that he might be planning to escape. His demeanor, coupled with the knowledge that no man had previously escaped the prison alive, caused the guards to soon relax any unusual vigilance toward him. He was treated as any other prisoner would be.

Being athletic, he finally won for himself a place on one of the prison baseball teams. On September 5, 1921, Labor Day, he participated in a baseball game against another team. About 3:30 p.m., while the game was in progress, he was observed by the guards to be moving at a speedy walk toward one of the barbed wire fences surrounding the playing field. He was followed by two other prisoners who were serving life sentences. Indeed, all three were moving in very unconcerned fashion and at first did not excite any unusual attention on the part of the guards until they reached the fence.

When called upon to halt, Gardner had already reached the fence. Drawing a pair of pliers from his pocket, Roy cut the wires and ran through the opening toward a patch of underbrush 50 yards away. He was followed by the other two inmates who served as a shield for him when the guards opened fire with their rifles. The other two prisoners dropped from the barrage of gunfire. Gardner, though he halted momentarily, as though wounded, continued his sprint for the brush and managed to gain cover. The prisoners who had been watching the game were cheering Roy on. Sensing there might be a mass escape, the guards stayed with the inmates.

As the pursuing guards reached the two fallen men, they were seen to be desperately wounded and were quickly removed to prison hospital. Every available guard was placed on Gardner's trail with Warden John Maloney taking personal charge of the search.

Roy was not found that night, or the next day. Although numerous people claimed to have seen him on the mainland, it was the belief of prison officials that he was hiding on the island waiting for an opportunity to swim to the mainland, or be picked up by a boat. An intensive search was conducted throughout the island and no boats were allowed to come within some distance for several days. A cordon of guards was maintained day and night around the entire island, but Gardner was not located.

But nothing was definitely known of Gardner's whereabouts until September 26 when George L. North, managing editor of the San Francisco *Call Bulletin* announced he had received two letters from Gardner, one detailing his escape from McNeil Island and the other an appeal to President Warren G. Harding to suspend sentences hanging over him in order that he might "make good" for his wife and daughter. Though postal authorities examined the envelopes in which the letters were received, the postmarks were illegible. Some doubt was at first expressed as to the authenticity of the letters, but close study of the handwriting convinced the officers the letters were actually written by Gardner.

With the knowledge that he had succeeded in reaching the mainland the officers directed every effort to recapture him. Numerous false leads all over the United States were followed to a conclusion. Reports were received that motorists had given rides to men they thought were Gardner, and others reported seeing men who answered his description and resembled the wanted posters. Though each and every clue was investigated, none led to Gardner and all proved false or cases of mistaken identity.

In his letter to North, Gardner stated he was wounded once in each leg and on reaching the underbrush, he concealed himself in a thicket, remaining there until after midnight when he crawled across a field to the prison barn. Roy said he climbed to the hayloft and hid under the hay, coming down each night to milk the cows. He remained there for over a week. Then he departed that security and crawled across the island until he reached the north end.

Once again concealing himself in a thicket, Gardner watched the boats all the next day and night and resolved that on the following night when the tide was at the ebb he would attempt to swim to Fox Island. Gardner claimed that although he was a strong swimmer, the swim to Fox Island was the most difficult he had ever made because the water was near freezing. Gardner stayed at Fox Island for four days, living off the milk of the farmers' cows and the apples in the orchards. In concluding the letter, Gardner refused to say where he had gone after leaving Fox Island, although he mentioned he stayed with someone who was willing "to put him up until his health was restored."

Gardner requested North to tell Dolly who had remained so loyal to him over the years not to worry and that

132

soon all would be all right. He swore that he had forsaken all future criminal activities and that if given an opportunity, he would atone for all his past deeds.

The plea to President Harding was forwarded by editor North who pleaded that Gardner was a criminal due to pressure on his brain from a metal plate placed there from an injury sustained at Bisbee while working in a mine back in 1908. Indeed, letters of sympathy followed North's public statement to the President. Harding did not bother to reply, although three weeks later Postmaster General J. Hayes issued a statement in which he said the government would not compromise with criminals.

Nothing further was heard of Gardner until November 15 when a man was arrested in Phoenix, Arizona, after he had attempted to rob a mail clerk in a railway mail car at the depot. The mail clerk, Herman Inderlied, was making up his mail pouches in preparation for his run, when he was confronted by an armed, masked man who ordered him to put his hands up and walk to the rear of the car. Reaching the back of the car, Inderlied was forced to lie down on his stomach. Seeing a chance to catch hold of the

Herman Inderlied

bandit's gun, Inderlied didn't hesitate to grab Gardner and wrestle him to the floor of the car, shouting for help at the same time. They fought viciously for a few minutes with Inderlied finally managing to sit on top of Gardner. He held Roy until help arrived.

After being taken to the police station, Gardner admitted his identity to the amazed officers. The search for the elusive mail robber had been completed once again and this time everyone hoped it would be the last.

In searching Gardner, articles stolen from a mail pouch at Maricopa, Arizona, a week earlier were found. Since it could be clearly shown that this crime was premeditated, Gardner was brought to trial on this charge. However, after a trial lasting a week, the jury was dismissed when they had deliberated for 72 hours without reaching a verdict. The United States Attorney prepared for a retrial, when Gardner's attorneys stated he would plead guilty to the Phoenix robbery if he could be given a light sentence. On December 18, 1921, Gardner entered the plea of guilty and was astonished to learn he received another 25 year sentence—this time to the United States penitentiary at Leavenworth, Kansas.

During his trial, Roy took the stand in his own behalf and claimed to have been moved by a spirit in all his criminal activities. This was accepted as an attempt to prove he was insane. After his arrival at Leavenworth in December 1921, he attempted to convince Warden Biddle of his insanity, but Biddle was unmoved.

Involved in several escape attempts at Leavenworth, Gardner was then transferred to the penitentiary in Atlanta in 1925. He remained there until 1934 when with a number of other prisoners considered dangerous or incorrigible, he was transferred under heavy guard to the new federal prison on Alcatraz Island in San Francisco Bay. Since the first weeks of his arrival, he had written to President Franklin Delano Roosevelt asking him to commute his sentence. Roosevelt never bothered to reply.

In the meantime, Dolly led several attempts to obtain his parole on the theory that a brain operation would restore him to normal mentality and remove his criminal tendencies. Other attempts for a parole and pardon were based on the grounds that during his criminal career he did not injure anyone. But all attempts were unsuccessful.

Gardner was finally pardoned in 1938, at which time he took various odd jobs in order to make a living. His wife Dolly had in the meantime remarried and was living in Napa. Roy settled down in a cheap hotel in the San Francisco Tenderloin and took a job at the Treasure Island Exposition as a barker advertising that "crime does not pay." Finally, at the end of his finances and extremely lonely, he committed suicide by inhaling potassium cyanide in his bathroom, making sure to leave a note for the maid the next morning not to enter the toilet since she might accidentally sniff some of the deadly fumes.

Gardner took his crimes and sensational escapes with a laugh. When captured, he would joke with the officers while discussing his misdeeds. He enjoyed recounting again and again the manner in which he had outwitted the authorities. His notoriety was a tragedy to Dolly who throughout his career as bandit and fugitive remained intensely loyal to him and their child. She spent 15 relentless years fighting for his parole, claiming he was mentally irresponsible for his crimes.

IX

The DeAutremont Brothers
at Tunnel 13:
Oregon's Great Train Robbery

The rainy weather that had plagued the Klamath Range of southern Oregon's Siskiyou Mountains had turned into a chilly drizzle that morning as the crack Southern Pacific Express pulled out of Ashland for its regular run to San Francisco. As the seven-passenger-car train slowly weaved up the mountain switchbacks toward the lonely Siskiyou Station at the top of the range, U.S. postal clerk Elvyn Dougherty casually began sorting the mail which had just been thrown on. Further back, passengers were sipping hot coffee and munching sandwiches. Winter had arrived early in 1923 and the cold, freezing weather found its way into the modern compartments. The story that was about to unfold would have stunned the best of mystery writers for its confusing plot, sensational worldwide hunt, and brilliant capture and trial of three young brothers.

Out of Ashland, the grade was steep to the remote station — a grade nearly 4 percent in places. Needed in such tortuous climbs were "helper" engines, coal burning steamers followed by oil fired engines. As train No. 13 arrived at 9:45 a.m., it pulled to a halt for two reasons. First, the "helper" had to be uncoupled and, second, the air brakes had to be tested before the train could be cleared for its downward descent into California. These

136

were standard Southern Pacific rules. When a southbound train left Siskiyou Station, it crawled along for about 100 yards at 5 to 8 miles per hour before it reached the 3,000-foot-long tunnel 13, a tunnel bearing the same ill-omened number as the train.

With the flying air test completed, the Baldwin locomotive slowly steamed through the muggy tunnel. At that moment, three men carrying sawed-off shotguns emerged from the bushes above the tunnel and jumped aboard the oil tender. Planning to rob the railway post office coach of its estimated $40,000, the three lay hidden until they could see the emerging light at the end of the tunnel. Roy DeAutremont, a 23-year-old twin brother, quickly crossed over to the engineer's cab and surprised the engineer and fireman with his raised shotgun.

"Halt this damn train when the mail coach comes out the bore!" he shouted.

Without hesitation, engineer Arnold Bates "big-holed" the brake handle as the first four cars emerged from the tunnel. Shoving the handle all the way against the stop, the compressed air shot through the lines clamping brake shoes against the wheels and at the same moment filling the air retaining tanks on every car. With a grinding, spark-flying, passenger-tumbling screech, the locomotive shuddered to a halt partly out of the tunnel. While passengers began to buzz with questions, Ray DeAutremont, the other twin, quickly ran across the track and affixed a package of dynamite to the door of the mail coach. At this moment, Dougherty, the mail clerk, poked his head out of the small window in the side door of his car. Hugh DeAutremont, the 19-year-old youngest of the three brothers, immediately leveled his shotgun and fired both barrels. But he missed, and Dougherty slammed the window shut, securing it with the safety bolt. Quickly, he began shoving loose furniture in front of the door.

In the meantime, the two bandits in the engine cabin forced the engineer and fireman to climb down on the

Locomotive which pulled Train

right-hand side of the gangway of the engine and stand in front of the locomotive. The DeAutremonts wanted them safe from the debris which was about to come from mail coach explosion. In later testimony, Roy DeAutremont said:

Ray gave the detonator a push and the mouth of the tunnel was rocked by a tremendous explosion. It was far stronger than we had planned. In fact, the blast was so severe that the mail clerk was blown to bits. I then took the fireman and started back down the track to uncouple the mail car. But the gassy and smokey air was too thick so I called for the fireman. The fireman and engineer were then marched toward the car. In a few seconds I saw someone coming with a red light from the passenger cars still in the tunnel. I shot at the man, who was a conductor, with my shotgun and at the same time Hugh shot him with his .45

No. 13 into Tunnel No. 13

Colt. The man staggered and I could see he was dying. Hugh walked over to him and shot him again, in cold blood. The engineer was put back up into the cab and Hugh told him to pull the main car ahead. He attempted to do this a number of times, but the engine wheels merely spun and the cars failed to move. Hugh then put the engineer back on the ground side next to the fireman while Ray and I looked the thing over to see what could be done about uncoupling the mail car and engine. But there was nothing we could do. So we walked back to the mail car and entered through the blown out front end. Our flashlights would not cut the steam and smoke so we left the mail car. Hugh in the meantime had ordered the engineer back into the cab. The fireman was standing alongside the engine with his arms in the air. Ray and I held a brief consultation as to what to do. We decided to kill the fireman. Ray shot him twice with the Colt. Hugh had the engineer covered and I shouted at him to bump him off and then we would clear out. We didn't want any witnesses. Hugh quickly shot the man in the head with his shotgun. We then fled to our cache which was between two and three miles northwest of the south entrance of the tunnel.

As the three brothers started running down the track, a second conductor and a passenger cautiously crept out of the tunnel to investigate the explosion and various gunshots. The two men were stunned by the sight. The conductor ran to an emergency phone near the tunnel and reported to police agents in Ashland. In turn, an agent in Ashland immediately notified Oregon sheriff's deputies and Dan O'Connell, chief special agent, in San Francisco.

While all this was going on, men were scrambling toward the tunnel from the nearby Siskiyou Station. The

D. O'Connell and M. F. McCarthy

explosion had rattled through the canyons and brought the four men on duty at the station to their feet. Train No. 13 was a passenger train and had apparently made an unscheduled stop in what was now a smoke-filled tunnel. In an instant, these four had rescue on their minds. When they reached it and saw the train intact, three men raced back and swarmed onto the sidetracked "helper." Quickly, they brought it to the tunnel entrance and coupled it with the caboose and shoved the stalled train out into the fresh air. It wasn't until the train had been shoved out that crew and passengers saw the bullet-punctured bodies of the two crewmen and the conductor. The mail car was still flaming. This car was immediately uncoupled. With the aid of a relief engineer, the original engine hauled the blazing car down the west side of the mountain to a bypass track at White Point. The "helper" then pulled the passenger cars back into Ashland.

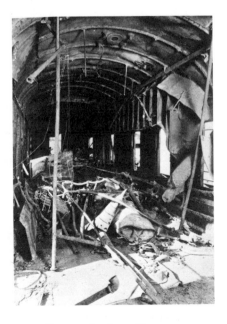

Dynamited mail car

By the time Dan O'Connell and other investigators arrived late that afternoon, the mail car had burned itself out. Among the ashes were found the human bones of the young redheaded mail clerk. O'Connell turned himself to the clues which were rapidly being found. Systematic searches by railroad personnel had turned up a .45 caliber Colt revolver and a DuPont blasting machine with a length of insulated wire running from it to the spot where the mail car had been blown up. Not far away was found a six-foot covering made out of gunny sacks and soaked in creosote, obviously to keep any bloodhounds off the trail. Three pack sacks lay near the foot-pads, apparently discarded when the bandits were forced to flee without a cent in booty. Now, with the sun setting, hundreds of men heavily armed and working in posses began scouring the

Siskiyou Mountain cabin of the
DeAutremont brothers

region. Bloodhounds were brought in and the government was planning on sending in planes to look for campfires that night. The next day they would fly above the rocky crags and thick growths of scrub pines at the top of the Siskiyous. A company of Oregon militia was hastily sent into action to aid in searching the vast mountain lowlands. O'Connell set up his headquarters at the nearby station and the next morning was happy to learn that two campsites and a small cabin had been discovered not far from the holdup scene. They yielded considerable evidence. It appeared that the bandits had used the cabin for three days prior to the robbery while making final plans. Special agents found a black traveling bag with a Railway Express shipping tag pasted on it near the railroad tracks about a mile south of the entrance to the tunnel. The major discovery, however, was a pair of greasy blue denim overalls. Its importance in identifying the three bandits would come a little later.

Overalls left at the scene

Several days passed as the manhunt increased. Even though dozens of suspects were rounded up and questioned, all had to be released for lack of evidence. O'Connell was sure that three men had participated in the murders, but there were no descriptions to send out. The overalls found near the tunnel had been examined thoroughly by various law enforcement agencies and railroad detectives, but no tangible evidence could be detected. On a hunch, O'Connell decided to send the overalls and other evidence to Dr. Edward Oscar Heinrich, a professor of chemistry at the University of California in Berkeley. Heinrich was considered a genius at scientific crime detection and had solved some important cases with next to nothing to work on.

Several days went by, O'Connell had received no word from the chemist. Meanwhile, he listened in depression to

Dr. Edward O. Heinrich

the official report that 20 sacks of regular mail and 150 pieces of registered mail had been destroyed in the mail car blast. Above all, he sat in quiet rage at the three cold-blooded killers who had murdered four innocent men— men who had been instructed to cooperate with robbers in cases such as this. As the days passed, the manhunters pressed all the harder in an effort to find some trace of the bandits. But all the trails lead to a dead end.

O'Connell was extremely pessimistic when the call finally arrived from professor Heinrich. The chief special agent was astonished when the scientist quietly said, "One of the men you are looking for is a left-handed lumberjack who had worked in the Northwest recently. He is about 25 years old, has brown hair, weighs about 165 lbs., and has a fair complexion. I believe he is about five feet, eight inches tall and he's rather fastidious in his personal habits."

O'Connell couldn't believe his ears. This was much more than he had expected—even from such a famed scientist. Heinrich then explained his findings, "There are streaks of fresh pitch on the overalls. They could have gotten there only by contact with pine trees. This, of course, suggests that our man is a lumberjack. I found Douglas fir needles in the pockets. This places him in the Northwest. A few strands of hair on the overalls tells us his color and also determines his approximate age." When O'Connell asked him to explain how he discovered the man was left-handed, Heinrich said, "There are worn places on the right side of the overalls but none on the left; so our man must have been standing with his right side against a tree while swinging an axe. This, of course, leads us to believe that he is left-handed."

"Well, it certainly looks as if you pinned him down to about everything except his name," laughed O'Connell.

"I believe his name is Roy DeAutremont," Heinrich quietly told the chief special agent. "I discovered a little piece of faded yellow paper jammed down in the narrow pencil pocket of the overalls. There appeared to be no writing on it, but under a microscope I detected some faint pen scratches. I brought them out under treatment in the lab. It turned out to be a receipt for a registered letter mailed by Roy DeAutremont at Eugene on September 14, 1923. It bore the number 236-L, and showed that $50 had been sent to Hugh DeAutremont at Lakewood, New Mexico."

O'Connell couldn't believe his ears! Never in the history of Southern Pacific investigations had so much been learned from so little evidence. Immediately he started the wheels rolling. A squad of detectives was dispatched to Eugene, Oregon, where they located an elderly barber, Paul DeAutremont, who told them he had three sons: Ray, Roy, and Hugh. Ray and Roy were 26 years old and twin brothers, while Hugh was the youngest at 18. The officers also learned from the father that Hugh had recently come north from Lakewood, New Mexico, where he had graduated from high school the previous June. He had joined his brothers and all three had been working as lumberjacks near Silverton, Oregon. Roy, the officers learned, was left-handed! The postal inspectors confiscated all of the brothers' clothing and personal effects.

Meanwhile, back at the University of California, Professor Heinrich continued to discover valuable information. Only three digits had been legible on the gun that was found at the holdup scene. However, Heinrich located the full set under the top strap of the revolver frame. The gun was traced to Seattle and was found to have been sold to a man who signed his name William Elliott. Handwriting analysis revealed that this was none other than Roy DeAutremont. Officers traced the purchasing of some of the kitchen utensils found in the cabin in the Siskiyous to the brothers. The express tag on the bag near the railroad tracks showed that Roy had shipped the bag at Eugene on January 21, 1923, to himself at Portland.

Armed with all this evidence, O'Connell and his agents were nonetheless frustrated because there was absolutely

$15,900 REWARD IN GOLD!

ROY A. A. DE AUTREMONT.
(Picture taken early in 1923.)

Roy A. A. DeAutremont, alias R. A. Harris, alias R. A Burton, age 23 in 1923; weight 135-140 pounds; height 5 feet 6 inches. Complexion medium light. Hair medium light brown. Eyes peculiar looking, narrow and squinty, light brown. Wears glasses in reading. Face broad at the cheek bones. Nervous, and a "dreamer." Likes to argue against the Bible. Long, turned up nose and prominent nostrils. Tonsils have been removed. Head round. Wears No. 6 shoe. Boastful and egotistical. Clips his words. Forward and presuming with women. First upper right molar tooth has amalgam filling, as have both first right and left lower molars.

RAY CHARLES DE AUTREMONT.
(Picture taken in 1920. He now resembles closely his twin brother Roy.)

Ray DeAutremont, alias R. C. Burton, alias William Elliott, alias Chas. R. Joseph, age 23 in 1923. Height 5 feet 6 inches. Weight 135-140 pounds. Complexion medium light. Hair medium light brown. Broad face. Prominent nostrils. Short cut neck. Eyes peculiar looking, light brown, small and squinty. Wears glasses when reading. Big toe nail on left foot turned up. Cut scar at tip of left forefinger inner, and at back of second joint right middle finger, also round cut scar back of head. Gold foil in upper left cuspid, mesail surface. Amalgam filling, upper left first molar, occlusal surface. Gold inlay, upper right cuspid, mesail and incisive angle.

HUGH DE AUTREMONT.
(Picture taken in 1923.)

Hugh DeAutremont, alias E. E. James, alias Hugh DeKay, alias Hugh DeLerious, alias Hugh DeCoy. Age 19 in 1923, looks older. Height 5 feet 7 inches. Weight about 135 pounds. Complexion fair, eyes blue. Nose slightly pug. Hair medium light, slightly sandy and curly. Amalgam filling right and left molars, and some in first right upper molar. Likes to argue and is good debater. Fond of sports, particularly boxing and running. Expressed desire for traveling, and has boasted of trips he has made by riding freight trains. He is bright and alert and has a high school education. Little fingers turn outward at first joint.

no sign of the brothers. They had vanished completely. The federal government offered a reward of $6,000 for the trio, the Southern Pacific offered $7,500, and the Railway Express Company offered $900. The brothers were reported to have been seen in nearly every part of the country, and though each of these leads was carefully checked out, the trails led nowhere. An incredible number of circulars were printed and distributed in Spanish, French, German, Dutch, and Portuguese. In all, 2,265,000 were sent throughout the world.

Dan O'Connell directed this worldwide hunt from his office at One Market Street in San Francisco. Charles Riddiford, chief postal inspector, was second in command in his office in Spokane, Washington. These two determined men spent long months running down every tip, every clue. With every opportunity, they kept interest alive in the minds of the public. Someone, somewhere would eventually recognize the badly wanted fugitives.

A year went by, then two. With the passing of the third year, a major development occurred. On a hot June night in 1926, Thomas Reynolds, a corporal in the army who had been stationed in the Philippines, walked into O'Connell's outer office and told the secretary that he had to speak immediately to the chief special agent.

O'Connell welcomed him into his office and Reynolds bluntly said, "I'm stationed on the Alcatraz Island Military Barracks, and last night I wandered into the Army post office and began looking over some old wanted posters tacked on the wall. I had nothing better to do just then and I found them interesting. All of a sudden I saw a familiar face. Under the name, Hugh DeAutremont, I recognized the picture as a man I once served with in Manila who called himself Jim Price."

O'Connell didn't bother to answer. He simply picked up the phone and within six hours "James C. Price" was arrested in Manila. Price astonished arresting officers by inquiring why it had taken them so long to discover his whereabouts. He readily admitted he was Hugh DeAutremont and without hesitation confessed to his role in the murders. Brought to San Francisco on March 17, 1927, he insisted he did not know the whereabouts of his brothers. The 23-year-old man was turned over to the state of Oregon and taken to Jacksonville to stand trial on the charge of murder in the first degree.

His capture was widely publicized and it helped stir up new interest in the hunt for the missing twin brothers. Radio stations broadcasted daily descriptions of Ray and Roy, while the U.S. Post Office printed and distributed an additional 75,000 "Wanted" posters.

Meanwhile, in Portsmouth, Ohio, elderly and crippled Albert Collingsworth, who was partially blind in one eye, read with interest the accounts of the Siskiyou holdup and search. The old man became excited as he noticed that the pictures of the DeAutremont twins closely resembled two men with whom he had worked at Hanging Rock. The two had called themselves Elmer and Clarence Goodwin.

Collingsworth promptly related his suspicions to the Maynard Detective Agency, who in turn notified the FBI.

DeAutremont twins at Steubenville, Ohio,
after their arrest

The "Goodwin" twins were arrested the following day on
June 8 in Steubenville, Ohio. Like their brother, they readily admitted their identity. However, they insisted they did
not kill the train's crew. They were extradited to Jacksonville and arrived there the day before Hugh went on trial.

The trial was a sensational and bizarre drama. Hugh was
not told of the capture of his brothers. When his trial
began the following day, many of his relatives were in the
Jacksonville courthouse. Professor Heinrich was the star
witness for the state and sharp cross-examination couldn't
discredit any of his conclusions. Meanwhile, the twins were
lodged in the old jail immediately adjacent to the courthouse and during the last day of Hugh's trial their voices
drifted through the open window. They were singing,
"You'll Never Miss Your Mother Till She's Gone."

That evening, the jury brought in a verdict of guilty, but
spared his life. Upon learning this, the twins decided to

plead guilty with the hope of also escaping the gallows. Hugh then admitted his part in the holdup. The guilty pleas accomplished their purpose and the brothers also received life sentences in the Oregon State Prison.

Roy, an outspoken optimist, stated he was the one who had thought up the robbery and had generally led his brothers in the attempt. He explained they were embittered toward society for sending Ray to prison some years earlier. It seems that Ray had served a year in the reformatory at Monroe, Washington, in 1919. He had been an enthusiastic worker for the I.W.W. and had held some sort of office for them. His activities with the "Wobblies" gained him the sentence, the offense being "syndicalism." Ray filled in the story on the twins' prolonged escape from custody. The two had escaped to Detroit within days of the murders. There, they worked for some time in major automobile plants. Ray married a young woman named Hazel Sprouse (she was present in the court room when he was sentenced) and changed his appearance by bleaching his hair blond with peroxide. He even had a gold tooth extracted when he learned in the wanted posters that this was one of his key facial characteristics. From Detroit, Ray and his young wife, moved to Hanging Rock, where they were followed a few months later by Roy. From there, the three moved to Steubenville. In the meantime, Hugh enlisted in the army in Chicago and volunteered for overseas duty.

The three brothers were sentenced to life imprisonment and dispatched to the state prison in Salem. Thomas Reynolds who had casually informed Dan O'Connell of Hugh's whereabouts received $5,300 of the total $15,900 reward money. Albert Collingsworth who recognized the twins was paid $1,700. Riddiford, nicknamed the "sly old fox" by journalists for directing the four-year search along with O'Connell said, "It cost the United States Government, Southern Pacific, and the American Express Company about a half million dollars to bring them to justice and every cent was well spent."

Nearly a third of a century passed before Hugh DeAutremont was granted a parole on November 24, 1958. The prison officials endorsed this move with the statement that he was "a testament to reformation." There were diehard Oregonians, however, who protested his release on the day it was granted. In prison, Hugh had learned the printing trade and following his release he went to work as a linotype operator in San Francisco. His newly acquired freedom didn't last long because he died of cancer in 1959, less than three months after his release.

Ray remained in prison where he taught Spanish, French, and Latin. He also became an accomplished painter and several of his imaginary landscapes won awards in state art exhibits. Roy, who officials acknowledged led his brothers in the tragedy was declared hopelessly insane. Transferred to the criminal ward of the Oregon State Hospital, he is still alive at this writing.

On October 11, 1961, the anniversary date of the now legendary Siskiyou holdup, the parole board voted in Ray's favor and he was released after 34 years behind bars. He would not disclose where he was headed, but when asked how it felt to be free, he smiled, "I'm trying to think of something to say, but can't. Well, you can imagine how it feels, can't you? But one thing is for sure: For the rest of my life I will struggle with the question of whatever possessed us to do such a thing."

X

Tom Vernon

The Southern Pacific West Coast Limited, Train No. 59, was clipping along at a speed of about twenty miles an hour around a curve near Saugus, California, late one evening in November 1929 when suddenly engineer Cyrus Ball felt the engine lurch. Immediately applying the emergency air, the train continued for a short distance, having left the rails and running along the ties. Then the engine, baggage car, and smoker turned over on one side severely scalding engineer Ball.

Immediately the passengers were in panic. Train crewmen rushed to the engine and removed the engineer from the cab. Company officials at Los Angeles were promptly notified, along with the railroad police department, the Los Angeles sheriff's office, chief of police of Burbank, and the local Southern Pacific doctor at Newhall. The doctor sped to the scene of the wreck, administering first aid to the engineer. Fortunately, he was not badly hurt.

Before the police arrived, conductor George French made a hurried check of all his passengers. Learning that none were hurt, he made an inspection of the rails at the point the train left the track. Nearby he discovered a claw bar and his inspection of the track revealed the derailment

The Coast Daylight

had been deliberate. The angle bars connecting the rails were removed and the spikes pulled from the track.

Several dazed passengers around the wreck noticed a man instructing them to climb back into the cars since arrangements had been made to tow the cars that had not been derailed back to Saugus. This occurred about 15 or 20 minutes after the derailment. When the passengers obeyed and returned to their Pullman cars at the rear of the train, the man adjusted a blue bandanna over his face, climbed aboard the second car from the rear, and produced a gun. Systematically robbing the passengers in the last two cars, the bandit casually said that he was a rancher in the vicinity and that all he wanted was money from the men. However, he took a purse from a lady passenger, which later proved to be a strong link in the evidence against him. He refused to take watches or jewelry. The holdup was completed without the knowledge of the train crew, although prior to the holdup, the bandit walked alongside the train speaking to several.

When the robber left the train, the passengers immediately started screaming. The train crew quickly began an intensive search for the bandit. The passengers revealed the bandit had secured about $200 from them. All roads in the vicinity were covered and the nearby rough country searched, although it was night.

The bandit was described as five feet, six or seven inches tall, about 40 years of age and weighing around 135 pounds. During the robbery he wore a blue bandanna with white circles or polka dots. Those passengers who had seen him prior to the holdup stated he had blue eyes, was smooth shaven, with a very thin face and sunken cheek bones and with a sharp nose. His clothing was described as a light suit of brown or gray, with the trousers being darker than the coat. One of the back pockets was torn in a triangular manner. His gun was described as a .32 or .58 revolver.

The Southern Pacific Company immediately authorized a reward of $5,000 for information leading directly to the

The engine of the West Coast Flyer
shortly after its derailment

arrest and conviction of each party involved in the derailment and robbery.

Chief special agent Dan O'Connell left for the scene that same night. The following morning, assisted by a corps of his own officers and the other police organizations, he conducted a close search of the territory. His investigation disclosed that the tools found at the scene were stolen from a nearby section tool house.

Members of the posse located the bandit's footprints leading from the right-of-way across rough ground toward the state highway. His gray coat was located about half a mile away. Nearby was the purse taken from the woman, along with a business card taken from a Southern Pacific passenger agent who was held up. Since the label in the coat showed it was made by a Cincinnati tailoring house, and there were cleaner's marks in the coat, efforts were promptly made to learn the identity of the owner of the coat.

Meanwhile, investigating officers learned that Thomas Frith, who was driving by the scene of the wreck in his automobile with his wife, two daughters, and a friend, had been approached by a man answering the description of the bandit. The man asked Frith for a ride into Los Angeles, stating he had been a passenger on the train and wanted to see his little daughter who had been injured and taken to the Children's Hospital in Hollywood. Frith told the stranger to get in his car and sped him to Hollywood.

Enroute to the hospital the man changed his story, telling the Friths he was a forest ranger and had been patrolling the hills on his horse. Noticing the wreck, he rode a short distance and since the hill was too steep for the horse, he climbed down on foot. He knew his little girl was on the train. Then the man changed this story again, saying the horse had sensed the wreck first, and plunged and snorted causing him to look down at the wreck. He claimed to have left his coat and horse on the hill in his hurry to get to his injured child whom he said was eleven years old. Although in confusion, the Frith family continued driving toward Hollywood.

Since the stranger looked somewhat familiar, Frith, who was employed in the motion picture studios, asked, "I believe I know you. What is your name?" "Hall," the stranger answered. The bandit then asked him if he was acquainted with several famous cowboys who he had worked with at rodeos and shows. He explained he was a native of Wyoming and had been working in Yellowstone, but had an operation for appendicitis and was sent to Santa Barbara. From there he made his way to Saugus.

On arrival at the hospital, he gave Frith $5 in payment for the ride and the Frith family said they would wait until he learned how his child was. He walked into the driveway of the hospital and disappeared from the sight. Returning in about five minutes, he said his girl's arms were broken, but her head was not crushed as he had feared. He said the nurse told him the child was under ether and no longer in danger. He explained he would stay in Hollywood that night. When asked where he lived, he said Willowbrook, which he said was between Compton and Watts. The bandit then asked Frith for his address. Mrs. Frith wrote it on the back of an envelope and gave it to him. The Friths then drove away and did not notice the direction in which the bandit walked.

When reading the accounts of the wreck and robbery on the following day, and noticing that the engineer was the only injured person in the wreck, they became suspicious and reported the matter to the Burbank Police Department

Investigation in Cincinnati revealed the coat that had been found near the wreck was sold to a man named Armstrong living in Pocatello, Idaho. Riley Armstrong, a well-known and respected resident of Pocatello, said he sold the coat to a secondhand dealer in May 1929. The cleaning marks in the coat were those of a Pocatello cleaners.

Hairs on the coat were examined in the laboratories of the Los Angeles Police Department. Experts revealed that the man had light hair and was about 40 years of age. Also, he was not very clean in his habits.

Several transients were suspected as being implicated in the crime, and one individual was particularly mentioned. A number of his friends identified the coat as being his property, but it was later proven they were mistaken because the fellow had been in jail at the time of the derailment. However, in his case, circumstances indicated he might be involved since he too was a former cowboy and rodeo star and knew all the persons mentioned to the Frith family by the bandit.

On November 25, 1929, one of Union Pacific's crack passenger trains was derailed near Cheyenne, Wyoming, and the passengers robbed by a lone bandit. This holdup was carried out in a manner similar to the wreck of the West Coast Limited and the descriptions given of the robber tallied in most details.

While the investigation was being handled by the railroad police and the robbery detail of the Los Angeles sheriff's office, Deputy Sheriff T. J. Higgins, who worked on the burglary detail, received a hint from E. G. Hewitt, an attorney in Los Angeles, that an exconvict whom they both knew might well be the party responsible. This convict known as Tom Vernon had been released from Folsom Prison in August 1929, and had stayed with Hewitt, acting as caretaker of his home until Hewitt discharged Vernon because he was disappearing at night and taking Hewitt's gun with him. Indeed, on one occasion he showed Hewitt a pair of rubber gloves from which he had cut off the right index, or trigger finger. When Vernon left, he stole Hewitt's revolver, clothing, and some money.

Deputy Higgins knew Vernon well. Vernon had helped the deputy during an attempted jail break a few years previous when Vernon was incarcerated in the Los Angeles County Jail. A man about 43 years of age, Vernon had by that time spent 22 years of his life in various prisons, having been convicted on six different felony charges. He had served terms in the Pennsylvania State Prison, Ohio State Prison, San Quentin Prison and three terms at Folsom Prison.

Deputy Higgins was immediately interested in the possibility that Vernon was the man wanted. He quickly secured his photograph and with his partner, Deputy Sheriff Bill Jones, contacted the officers working on the case. Sheriff Traeger assigned Deputies Higgins and Jones to check on the lead. The photograph, along with several other photographs of different convicts, was shown the Frith family. They immediately picked out Vernon as the man who rode in their car. It was learned that Vernon had been a stockman and rodeo performer when not in prison. With this break, the photograph was shown to members of the traincrew and passengers, who quickly identified him.

A day later, attorney Hewitt and his stenographer, Miss Elsie Serrano, and Deputy Higgins each received a letter from Vernon, postmarked in Cheyenne. In each of the letters, he mentioned he left Los Angeles on a truck on the morning of November 10 enroute to Denver. Officers felt he mentioned this point in each of the three letters in order to establish an alibi in case he was suspected of the train wrecking and robbery.

When the information was received that the Union Pacific train had been wrecked and the passengers robbed near Cheyenne, it was immediately believed that Vernon was responsible for both crimes.

The information was laid before a special session of the grand jury of Los Angeles County on November 26, 1929, the day following the Union Pacific wreck. The Grand Jury returned an indictment charging Vernon with train wrecking.

In the meantime, Deputy Sheriff Higgins was rushed to Denver. Higgins discovered Vernon had stayed at the Manx Hotel before moving on to Cheyenne. But when the employees of the hotel were questioned, one of the chambermaids produced a note left by Vernon which read, "House Maid, if I can ever help you, write me." This note was signed "Buffalo Tom Vernon, Pawnee, Oklahoma, care of Pawnee Bill's Buffalo Ranch."

With this new lead, Higgins, who now was joined by Sheriff D. Romas of Cheyenne and special agent Matt McCourt of the Union Pacific, rushed to Pawnee and placed Vernon under arrest without trouble.

On December 2, 1929 Vernon confessed that he had derailed train No. 59 and robbed the passengers, although he denied any participation in the Union Pacific wreck and robbery. However, the Union Pacific officers and the sheriff from Cheyenne felt they had too strong a case against him and promptly filed a requisition for him with the governor of Oklahoma.

A new indictment charging Vernon with train wrecking and four separate counts of robbery was returned by the Los Angeles grand jury on December 4 and extradition papers were signed by Governor Young and forwarded by air mail to the governor of Oklahoma.

In the meantime, alibis which Vernon might have offered for having left Los Angeles on the morning of November 10 were dashed by the discovery of people he visited late that night in Los Angeles. He had purchased several bundles of flowers for a woman in a Los Angeles hospital; but since it was too late at night, he was asked to bring them in the following morning. Officers learned he did return to the hospital on the morning of November 11 with the flowers for the lady.

With Wyoming officers pressing for the return of Vernon to their state, Deputy Higgins wired California from Oklahoma City, requesting that everything possible be done to assure Vernon being returned there. Attorney General Webb of California wired the attorney general of Oklahoma that California had a conviction positively assured. District attorney Buron Fitts of Los Angeles County was notified that a hearing was to be held in the governor's office at Oklahoma City, December 7. Chartering an airplane on December 6, he flew to Oklahoma City arriving in time for the hearing.

The hearing was attended by Governor William J. Holloway of Oklahoma; the governor's attorney, Baxter Taylor; County Attorney Allan Picket of Cheyenne; Sheriff Romsa of Cheyenne; special agent Matt McCourt of the Union Pacific; District Attorney William Fitts of Los Angeles and Deputy Sheriff Higgins of Los Angeles. The facts of the West Coast Limited derailment were outlined by Fitts, while presenting the mass of evidence connecting Vernon with the crime. He concluded with Vernon's confession. He also induced Sheriff Jones of Pawnee to testify that he had arrested the bandit for the California officers, thus giving them a prior right to Vernon. The Wyoming case was also presented, but they admitted Vernon denied any participation in their wreck and robbery.

At the conclusion of the hearing, Governor Holloway decided Vernon should be returned to California. He was returned on that same day by Deputy Higgins, arriving by train in Los Angeles on December 9, 1929. After his arrival in Los Angeles, he was thoroughly questioned by Dan O'Connell, Captain James Brooks of the Sheriff's office, and other officers working on the case. He made another complete confession, and when taken to the scene of the crime pointed to the place where he had tampered with the rail, showing where he had waited for the train to pass.

While the extradition question was being threshed out in Oklahoma, officers were active back in California. Deputy Higgins learned from Vernon that he had been given a coat when leaving Folsom in August. The coat was taken to the prison and there identified as being the coat of a suit

Tom Vernon

Tom Vernon (seated) with
railroad detective Tom Higgins

given Vernon. This coat was purchased from the second-hand dealer at Pocatello by another prisoner who identified it. When this second prisoner was sentenced to Folsom the suit was placed in the prison wardrobe and given to Vernon when he was released. Thus, another definite link in the chain of evidence was forged against Vernon.

On December 12, Vernon appeared in the superior court of Los Angeles before Judge Aggeler. He entered a plea of guilty to two additional counts of robbery. He was represented by Public Defender Eugene Davis. Davis asked the Court to appoint alienists to examine Vernon's mental and physical condition. Since his prison record revealed the notation, "Syphiletic, Cured." Davis felt that Vernon might be insane. The Court appointed three doctors to examine Vernon and report back on December 17. The doctors reported that Vernon was entirely sane within the meaning of the law and responsible for his acts.

On December 18, Judge Aggeler sentenced Vernon to serve life imprisonment in the California State Prison at Folsom without hope of parole on the train wrecking charge; life imprisonment under the California Habitual Criminal Act, and five years to life on the robbery charge. Before sentence was passed, District Attorney Fitts made a plea that Vernon be given the death sentence. At this time Vernon was represented by attorney John Cooper of Los Angeles who had been hired by Major G. W. Lillie, otherwise known as "Pawnee Bill." Vernon had at one time worked for him.

Vernon was returned to Folsom Prison and given back his old job of hoist engineer. A short time later, he began writing letters stating he had been "framed." However, every time he was convicted, he made the same contention and the charge was not taken seriously.

Vernon's early history was quite interesting. He claimed to have been the son of James and "Cattle Kate" Averill who were hanged as cattle rustlers in Wyoming when he was a small boy. He grew up around ranches and was a cowboy and rodeo performer.

Thus the Vernon case was closed. Tom Vernon, seven times convicted of felonies, always complained he never had a chance. Confined in Folsom for the rest of his natural life, he seemed at home, behaving as a "model inmate." Vernon's plea for *habeas corpus* was denied in May 1947 by the California State Supreme Court.

XI

The Lamar Wolf Pack

The unmasked, heavily armed man worked with quiet deliberation as the early morning darkness gradually turned into dim light. It was going to be another warm June day in 1929 and the man had a great deal to do in the few minutes available to him. Train No. 36 was due and he had to unload the heavy-duty World War I machine gun from the trunk of his old Hudson touring car and assemble it alongside the railroad tracks.

As the man finished fitting the pieces together on that lonely stretch between Pittsburg and Port Chicago in California's Contra Costa County, two well-dressed men were boarding the passenger train seven miles down the road at Bay Point. One man carried a large denim sack folded over with some obviously long objects in it. As the two gave the conductor their tickets to Pittsburg, the man assembling the heavy weapon finished and threw a canvas tarp over it. He quickly retreated into some nearby bushes and placed a mask over his face.

Sitting in the rear seat of a partitioned coach, the two passengers looked out the window in the increasing morning light and watched until they spotted their signal down the track. A few moments later when the train approached the small, non-agency station of McAvoy, the two quickly

163

pulled out automatic pistols and fired several shots into the floor. Attracting a great deal of attention, the conductor ran into the coach where he was captured. He was ordered to quickly give the stop signal to the engineer. As he proceeded to do this, the other bandit rounded up twelve passengers, two conductors, and a brakesman. Held at gunpoint, they were then ordered to march toward the forward end of the car. When the train pulled to a hurried stop, one of the robbers took charge of the passengers and trainmen, while the other hurried to the engine cab. Marched to a small, shallow depression between the tracks and fence, they were ordered to be seated with their hands on their heads. The bandit then opened the sack he was carrying and pulled out several sections of a Thompson submachine gun and assembled it. In the meantime, the third robber emerged from the bushes and threw off the tarp of the heavy weapon and stood guard directly behind the train several hundred yards away.

As the second man started boarding the locomotive, engineer Joe Barnes and fireman Bob Jensen, who were curious why they had been signaled to stop in such a desolate area, were startled by a stern order to throw up their hands. Flourishing his automatic at the trainmen, the bandit started climbing the ladder into the cab. But Barnes quickly reached over and grabbed the gun. Attempting to wrestle it away, the bandit pulled back and shot the engineer at point-blank range. Fortunately, the bullet lodged between the elbow and shoulder of Barnes' left arm. Although a painful wound, it was not serious. The bandit then clambered aboard and into the engine cab. As he did so, the fireman fled into the pilot of the engine. Bleeding and almost fainting, Barnes was shoved down the ladder and across to where the other trainmen and passengers were sitting. The bandit then placed the train in reverse and backed it to where the third robber was waiting with his heavy machine gun, stopping the train when the mail coach was directly opposite the gun. Nearby, the auto was parked on a dirt road leading from the right-of-way to the main highway.

With the locomotive at a standstill, the bandit in the engine cab quickly put the fire out and let the steam out of the boiler. He jumped from the cab, ran back to where the passengers and trainmen were held and selected conductor Fred Wamsley to accompany him to the mail car. As they jogged down the line, the bandit spotted the fireman sneaking through the bushes to the highway. A pistol shot abruptly stopped him. He raised his hands and walked toward the bandit and conductor.

When express messenger Lucius Allen realized a holdup was taking place, he closed the door of his car. Reaching the car door, Wamsley and the fireman were ordered to knock and demand that it be opened. In response, Allen slid the door open a fraction, peering into the morning light. The bandit raced up and leveled his automatic at him, instructing him to put his hands up. Allen did as he was ordered and the bandit jumped aboard, as the bandit with the machine gun covered the conductor and fireman, as well as any other who might wonder what was going on Inside the mail car, the robber was ransacking everything. Finding only a small package of cheap jewelry, the man cursed and muttered something about being double-crossed on the "big shipment." Then, he turned and ordered Allen from the coach.

Shoving the three men in front of him, the bandit proceeded to a second mail car and shouted to mail clerk Ralph Tyler to open the door and throw down the registered mail. Tyler shouted back that he most certainly would not, and besides he didn't have any valuables. At that point, the bandit motioned for the three trainmen to move back a few yards and then ordered his partner to blast the front of the coach. A thundrous din shattered the quiet morning as 200 bullets ripped into the wooden door, splintering it to kindling. With the door hanging from its hinges, the bandit walked over to him and fired a single shot past his head, saying that he would blow his goddam head off if he didn't turn over the Pittsburg steel plant payrolls. Tyler got up and without a word passed several keys over and motioned to the neatly piled sacks stacked on a special rack across the coach. After placing all the pouches into a small wooden box lying near by, the bandit demanded to know if that was all. Tyler said he wouldn't double-cross him after having survived such an experience. The bandit laughed and told him to stay where he was. He then jumped from the car and ordered the three trainmen to enter and not come out for a full ten minutes or they would be killed.

The two bandits then abandoned the heavy machine gun and raced back down the track to where their partner was holding the others hostage by the automobile. When they reached the small group, the bandits ordered them to walk back to the train at a casual pace and no one would be hurt. As the passengers and trainmen scrambled to their feet and started down the track, the three bandits climbed through the fence and got into their old Hudson touring car. Starting the motor, the bandits fled down the dirt road as fast as the car would travel. In their bags were $19,000 in cash.

Conductor Wamsley was able to flag down a Sacramento Northern train a few minutes later. On this train was a portable telephone and Wamsley was able to inform postal authorities in Pittsburg within 20 minutes of the robbery. They in turn notified Sheriff Veale's office in Martinez and Southern Pacific officials at the Oakland Pier. By 10:30 a.m. that morning, a cordon of armed police carrying sawed-off shotguns encircled the entire central part of California.

The first major clue officers received came in later that afternoon when it was discovered that the old Hudson auto had been set afire at an abandoned lime and cement plant on a back road between Bay Point and Concord.

Converging there, the officers learned that the car had been saturated with gasoline and dynamited. Checking with every known farmer or rancher in the vicinity, it was also discovered that when the auto was deserted, three men left the scene in what appeared to be a Chevrolet or Overland coupe driven by a woman. Detectives also learned later that afternoon that the Hudson had been

Circular No. 213

$9900.00 REWARD

Southern Pacific Mail and Express Train No. 36 was held up about 1¼ miles east of McAvoy, Contra Costa County, California, 8:45 A. M., June 22nd, 1929, by two men, who boarded the train at Bay Point. After train left the station the bandits pulled guns and held up the conductor, brakeman and passengers, forcing the conductor to signal the engineer to stop the train.

When the train stopped one of the bandits got off, going forward to the engine. The engineer scuffled with the bandit for the gun and was shot in the left arm. The bandit then forced the engineer to back the train to where bandits had an old dark colored Hudson super-six seven passenger touring car, California License 7 T 50 86, parked.

Passengers were forced to detrain and were left in custody of bandit No. 2 who used what appeared to be a machine gun. Bandit No. 1 forced conductor to go to mail and express car making clerk and messenger to open doors and come out. The bandit then entered the car and soon left with two mail pouches containing loot of $16,000.00 in currency.

At the point where bandits abandoned the Hudson automobile they left in coupe automobile which contained a woman.

DESCRIPTIONS:

No. 1	No. 2	No. 3. Woman
Age: About 32 years	Age: About 40 years	Age: About 40 years
Height: About 5 ft. 7 in.	Height: About 5 ft. 8 in.	Height: About 5 ft 7 in.
Weight: About 145 lbs.	Weight: About 150 lbs.	Weight: About 120 lbs.
Hair: Dark	Hair: Dark Brown	Hair: Dark Brown
Eyes: Brown	Eyes: Blue Gray	Eyes: Dark Brown
Complex: Medium Dark	Complex: Medium	Complex: Medium.
Wore sun glasses	Wore sun glasses	
Supposed to have mole on cheek.	Supposed to have scar on eyebrow.	

The above reward will be paid for information leading directly to the arrest and conviction of the guilty persons. United States Post Office Department $2000 each, Southern Pacific Company $1000.00 each, Railway Express Agency Inc. $300.00 each. If all three are convicted $9900.00.

Wire all information to me at my expense.

R. R. VEALE, Sheriff, Contra Costa County,
MARTINEZ, CALIFORNIA
TELEPHONE MARTINEZ 81

OR NOTIFY: C. E. Caine, Post Office Inspector in Charge, San Francisco, California.

D. O'Connell, Chief Special Agent, Southern Pacific Co., 65 Market Street, San Francisco, California.

W. C. Rutherford, Chief Special Agent, Railway Express Agency Inc., San Francisco, California.

Dated: Martinez, California, June 29th, 1929.

purchased from a used car dealer in Los Angeles a few days before. All available Southern Pacific special agents were assigned to trace this new clue.

The next morning, with the first excitement of the sensational story past, officers from the railroad, post office, and sheriffs' departments, including representatives of the FBI, conferred and laid out their plans of strategy. During that conference, a call came through to chief special agent Dan O'Connell from Clarance Morrill, superintendent of the State Bureau of Criminal Investigation, that two men and a woman had been arrested a few months before on vagrancy charges, although Stockton authorities had learned the three were planning to rob the payroll for the Pittsburg steel mills. The suspects were identified as W. H. Holden, Joe Miller, and Betty Wright. O'Connell's investigation revealed that Holden was known to railroad officers under the aliases of Warren, Ryan, and Reed, although his true name was William Harrison Fleagle. Jake Fleagle had been involved in a series of box car burglaries on the Santa Fe Railroad in 1922, but had managed to escape. Very little was discovered about Joe Miller, except that he was a butcher by trade who spent more time gambling than working. The woman was known as Betty Gramps, Betty Wright, and Betty Holden, although in fact she was Fleagle's wife.

But the descriptions of Fleagle and Miller tallied in a general way with the descriptions of the train robbers. To substantiate the belief that this was indeed the gang involved, Morrill said that when Fleagle and Miller were arrested in Stockton, a veritable arsenal had been found in their residence.

Meanwhile, checking on the abandoned Hudson, detectives learned that it had been bought by a party signing the sales contract as James Hendrix, or James Henderson. From the description furnished of the man, O'Connell believed that this was the third bandit and that he was an intimate friend of Fleagle's, Dr. C. O. DeMoss who had

Betty Gramps

deserted his practice in order to become a full-time gambler. DeMoss had worked as a card dealer in various Tracy, California, gambling houses.

Several weeks passed without clues or tips regarding the gang's whereabouts. Good citizens, amateur detectives, and enterprising reporters poured "clues" and sightings into O'Connell's office. Although every "tip" was followed faithfully, nothing dramatic turned up.

On July 6, 1929, the third major break in the case occurred. In a canyon about twenty miles east of Hollister on the Pacheco Pass Highway, the mail sack in which the plunder had been carried was found. This mail sack was concealed in a gunny sack and was discovered accidentally by a state highway employee. There were a number of torn letters, three currency bags, and several bank wrappers in the sack indicating the bag contained the full $19,000.

The gunny sack in which the mail bag was concealed had been made for a San Francisco sugar refinery. Efforts to trace it through marks on it were unsuccessful. Due to the condition of the letters, it was impossible to state how long since the sack had been opened. In the immediate vicinity two cigarettes of a foreign make and a short length of dynamite fuse were found. Neither of these clues yielded any results.

When Fleagle was arrested in Stockton on the vagrancy charge and later released because of lack of evidence, his fingerprints were taken and he was photographed in the routine manner. The fingerprints were sent to the Federal Bureau of Investigation in Washington, D.C. The FBI was able to inform O'Connell that Fleagle had a record in Oklahoma for train robbery.

On July 19, word was received that Joe Miller had been arrested in Reno and admitted his friendship with Jake Fleagle, although denying any complicity in the train robbery. Although intensively interrogated, he refused any knowledge of the holdup. He had been working in a nearby mining camp as a waiter and lived in a small Japanese hotel in Reno. Miller insisted he had been in his room on the night of the robbery, although no one in the hotel remembered seeing him.

California authorities decided to bring Miller to San Jose, California, to answer an earlier charge of robbery. Several months previous to the holdup, Miller, Fleagle, and DeMoss had robbed Tom Jenkins of $1,400. While incarcerated, passengers and train crew visited Miller and there was equal division of opinion regarding Miller's role in the train robbery. Conductor Wamsley who had the best opportunity to scrutinize all three bandits was especially emphatic that Miller was not one of the robbers.

In the meantime, O'Connell received information that the fingerprints of Jake Fleagle had been found to compare exactly with the fingerprints left on the automobile of Dr. W. W. Winegar of Dighton, Kansas, who had been kidnapped from his home on May 23, 1928, to aid one of the bandits wounded in a holdup of the First National Bank of Lamar, Colorado. After treating the gangster's wounds, Dr. Winegar was murdered in cold blood and his body left in his own automobile at the foot of a cliff. This information was indeed sensational.

The Lamar Wolf Pack

The discovery that Fleagle's fingerprints matched the latent prints found on the murdered man's car was the first direct clue to the identity of the bank robbers the officers investigating that crime had received in over a year's search. Two other suspects were being held in the Dighton jail for investigation of murder, even though Fleagle's identity was known.

The Lamar robbery was one of the most violent crimes ever committed in the Rocky Mountain states. As the county seat of Prowers County, Lamar was a small farming community in the southeastern corner of Colorado not far from the Kansas line. At 1:15 p.m. on the warm afternoon of May 23, 1928, four gangsters entered the First National Bank and promptly killed the president and his son. A. N. Parrish, the 70-year-old president, had reached for a loaded pistol that for many years had been kept in the top drawer of his desk. Without hesitation, Parrish jerked out his revolver and shot one of the bandits in the face, the bullet ripping away part of his jaw. The banker was then riddled in a withering fire by the gangsters. As the son rushed to his father, the robbers blasted him.

Despite the profuse bleeding from his face, the wounded bandit gathered money from the tellers' cages. This gangster was described as about five feet, ten inches tall, heavy set, ruddy complexion, a round face and about 35 years of age.

Despite the barrage of gunfire and the alarm given, the gangsters quickly gathered up the available money and securities, totalling $22,500, of which $13,700 was in cash and $12,400 in Liberty Bonds. Then the robbers retreated. Two bank employees were kidnapped as shields in case the bandits were trapped. Running rapidly down the street, they jumped into a large Buick sedan and drove away at a high rate of speed.

Sheriff L. E. Alderman was notified of the holdup and immediately pursued in his own auto. The trail led over several crossroads until it led back to the main highway

171

leading north and east. About fifteen miles from Lamar, the gangsters noticed that the sheriff was catching up with them. Stopping the car, they shoved one of the bank employees from the car. Continuing on for a few more miles, the sheriff gained on them once again and again they halted, this time at the foot of a hill expecting the sheriff to drive past them. Observing this, Sheriff Alderman made a quick stop, jumped from his car and using a ditch for protection opened fire on the outlaws. They answered with high-powered rifles, riddling his car with bullets. Since the sheriff only had his revolver and a shotgun, he was at a disadvantage. After a few minutes of hot gunfire, the bandits returned to their car, and sped away. When the sheriff attempted to renew the pursuit, he found his auto had been disabled by their bullets.

But this temporary setback did not deter Alderman. Later that day, he formed several heavily armed posses and scoured the hills near the Kansas border. One of the posses located the trail of the outlaw car leading into Kansas through isolated hills, gullies, and box canyons. The trail was lost at nightfall, in the Smoky Hill River country.

During the night, Dr. William Winegar of Dighton, Kansas, was telephoned into the country on the pretext that a youth had been injured in a tractor accident. Winegar was the type of general practitioner who responded to all calls at any hour. Gathering instruments into his bag, he drove out to a small ranch. Winegar never returned. Thirty six hours later his body was found in his auto, having been shot in the head with a shotgun.

The body of Kessinger, the second bank employee kidnapped, was found three weeks later in an abandoned cabin in the Sand Hills near Liberal, Kansas. He had been riddled with pistol bullets and the gun used was discarded in a corner of the cabin.

When Winegar's automobile was found, Sheriff Alderman felt fingerprints might be found on the auto that might lead to the identification of the killers. With this in mind, he ordered a guard posted around the death car and quickly flew to Garden City, Kansas, where he secured the services of James Twilliger, fingerprint expert of the Garden City Police Department. Returning with Twilliger, the auto was carefully analyzed for prints and it was discovered the car had been carefully wiped both inside and out of all finger marks. However, a thorough search resulted in the development of one distinct fingerprint on a rear window. A photograph of this print was taken and forwarded to the FBI in Washington, D.C., with the result it was identified as the thumbprint of Jake Fleagle.

The Colorado and Kansas authorities checked on the Fleagle family in Kansas and found they had been operating a "horseless" horse ranch of 160 acres. With the exception of the home and a large garage nearby, the property had been allowed to fall into decreptitude. Sheriff Alderman and Chief of Police John Richardson, of Garden City, Kansas, drove to the ranch, where the father and mother of the Fleagle boys lived. This family had been in that part of the country over 40 years. It was learned from neighbors that in 14 years not one acre of ground had been cultivated. There were four sons in the Fleagle family, Walter, Fred, Ralph, and William, who was known as "Little Jake."

Walter was married and living with his wife and two children on a farm about two miles from his father's place. Fred lived with the father. Ralph and Jake were supposed to be traveling in California. In addition, the officers learned that though neither the elder Fleagle's ranch nor Walter's farm were cultivated, both appeared to be well off financially. The families never associated with anyone, and neighbors strongly suspected them of being bootleggers and still operators.

It was decided to place the Fleagles under arrest. The father, Walter, and Fred were taken to the city jail at Garden City. After their arrest, it was discovered the Fleagles had post office boxes in Garden City and Dodge City under assumed names. They had received packages of money through these boxes. $150,000 was found to be on deposit in Garden City banks in their accounts during the previous nine years. They recently had over $60,000 on deposit, although it was suddenly withdrawn. A check in Dodge City showed they had $10,000 on deposit. It was also discovered that they had several thousand dollars in banks in Scott City.

The arrest of the Fleagles was kept secret and the various post office boxes were placed on close surveillance. A day or two after the arrest a letter postmarked Kankakee, Illinois, arrived from Ralph Fleagle. Sheriff Alderman immediately went to Kankakee and explained to the postmaster who he was. He then took a vigil where he could observe anyone coming to the general delivery window. Within fifteen minutes, a man walked up to the window. Alderman quickly recognized Ralph Fleagle, because of his resemblance to his two brothers. Following Ralph from the post office, the Sheriff saw him visit a bank and telephoned the local police department for help. Within ten minutes, Ralph Fleagle was placed under arrest. A safe deposit box was located in which was found $1,200 in cash and $6,500 in Liberty Bonds, none of which corresponded with the Liberty Bonds stolen from the Lamar Bank. In Ralph's automobile, which bore Illinois plates, a set of California license plates were found under the seat, as well as three revolvers and 140 round of ammunition.

That day a telephone call from Peoria, Illinois, was received at the hotel where Ralph had been living under an alias. The caller asked that when Ralph returned the operator ask him to call a certain party at a given address in Peoria. Sheriff Alderman telephoned the Peoria police who promptly arrested a man and a woman at the address. When the man saw the police officers, he attempted to jump into an automobile and flee. Sheriff Alderman rushed to Peoria, arriving shortly after the arrests. He did not know the man arrested, who had given his name as Dr.

G. O. DeMoss. DeMoss was questioned about his connections with the Fleagles, but the Sheriff could not get enough evidence to link him with the bank robbery and he was released. But when Alderman had an opportunity to see the auto in which DeMoss attempted to escape, his heart leaped. It was the blue Master Six Buick Sedan used in the Lamar holdup. The sheriff knew where the car had been stolen prior to the bank robbery and had the engine number. However, all traces of the auto were lost when the bandits made their escape.

Although the woman had been questioned and released, it was learned she had warned Jake Fleagle who was in Peoria with them. Jake had fled in such a hurry that he left his hat behind. The apartment occupied by "Little Jake," DeMoss, and the woman, was searched, yielding five rifles, an automatic shotgun, four pistols, and 2,000 rounds of cartridges.

Ralph Fleagle was brought to Garden City and there sufficient evidence was gathered to insure his prompt conviction of the Lamar robbery and murders. Fleagle was aware of this and also knew of the determined efforts being made to locate his brother Jake. Photographs and descriptions of his younger brother were distributed throughout the United States, Canada, and Mexico.

The officers investigating the train robbery furnished Sheriff Alderman with considerable information as to the operations of Ralph and Jake as boxcar burglars on the Pacific Coast. Moreover, they learned that the Liberty Bonds furnished as bail for Jake, Joe Miller, and Betty Gramps, when arrested in Stockton, were a part of the Lamar loot. They also learned that Ralph Fleagle had cashed several Liberty Bonds in the Bank of America in San Francisco, thus connecting Ralph not only with the robbery and murders, but with the disposition of the securities stolen.

On Friday, August 9, 1929, Ralph Fleagle confessed. He implicated his brother Jake and three other men named Howard L. Royston, George J. Abshier alias Bill Messick, and Ernest Rhoda. This gang of boxcar burglars operated on the Pacific Coast. It was revealed that Royston was the bandit who was wounded and that Ralph called Dr. Winegar to drive out and attend him. Ralph prepared a fake note which would indicate revenge was the motive for the murder of Winegar and left it near the body, although Jake did the actual killing.

Ralph's confession told of taking Royston to Salina, Kansas, and from there to St. Paul, Minnesota, where he received treatment in a hospital for his wound. Ralph and Jake then drove out to California and Messick remained with Royston for about a month. Royston also decided to drive to California where he had been employed by a cement concern in San Andreas. But, in August 1928, he worked for three days and it became necessary for him to return to St. Paul for further treatment. Ralph Fleagle stated that in September 1928, he, Jake, and Messick disposed of a large portion of the stolen Liberty Bonds through the Bank of Italy in San Francisco. The agreement between the gang was that Royston and Abshier were each to receive one-eighth of the loot, equivalent to $27,000.

On the day Royston was to leave San Andreas for St. Paul, he was arrested and brought back to Lamar. The officers working on the train robbery questioned him, but he would reveal nothing. Abshier was arrested in Grand Junction, Colorado, where he had long been known as a liquor dealer and resort keeper. Jake still managed to elude the authorities and his whereabouts was unknown. After Ralph Fleagle's confession, for which he was promised that the prosecution would not ask for the death penalty, his father and two brothers were released.

Shortly afterwards, Dan O'Connell arrived in Lamar to question Ralph Fleagle, Royston, and Abshier about the train robbery. But before leaving the Bay Area, O'Connell called on Royston's mother in San Andreas. Mrs. Royston said she too would visit her son, but in the meantime to

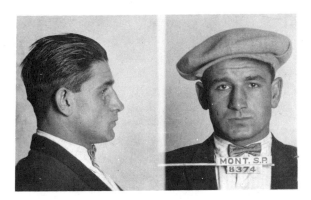

George Abshier

Ernest Rhoda

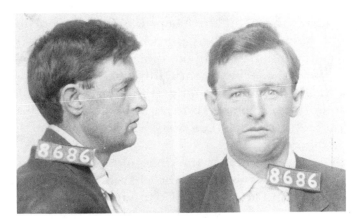

Howard L. Royston

please deliver a letter asking that he make a clean breast of everything. Mrs. Royston included a photograph of his dead father, a former San Francisco police officer. She blamed Henry Ryan, the alias under which she knew Jake, for the trouble her son was in.

On September 18, 1929, O'Connell, Sheriff Alderman, and Tim O'Leary, superintendent of special service of the Santa Fe, questioned the three bandits. Royston and Abshier had already admitted participation in the Lamar robbery, but would not offer details. Now, when closely questioned concerning their movements, they refused to admit any connection with the train robbery. But in an effort to obtain clemency for themselves, they confessed five other bank robberies in which the Fleagle gang were involved. The proceeds of these robberies totaled $307,250, which in addition to the Lamar loot, made the total amount almost half a million dollars in six years of activity.

While freely detailing their bank robberies in Kansas and Colorado, Royston and Abshier denied any knowledge of the train holdup, other than what they read in the newspapers. However, when O'Connell gave Royston the letter from his mother and said she was about to see him, Royston hinted that Jake was connected with the post office robbery there. That robbery was suspected of having been committed by the gang which robbed train No. 36. Abshier mentioned that Jake spoke of a train job. After seven different interviews with Royston, O'Connell was convinced that he knew nothing of the train robbery, but was not so certain about Abshier. Royston also disclosed that Ernest Rhoda, alias Lee Solliers, had participated in some of these crimes.

Ralph Fleagle, Howard, Royston, and George Abshier all entered pleas of guilty to the charge of first degree murder in the district court of Colorado. Since the law in Colorado was that a jury must pass on a murder judgement, juries were empaneled with District Judge Oscar

Hollenbeck presiding. On October 8, 1929, Abshier's trial started and on October 12 he was found guilty of murder in the first degree. He was sentenced to hang. Royston was also found guilty and sentenced to hang on October 16.

On October 22, 1929, Ralph Fleagle's trial began and the moot question of immunity entered. Fleagle's counsel contended the prosecution had guaranteed him life imprisonment in return for his confession. However, on October 26, he was found guilty and the jury recommended the death penalty thereby making it mandatory for the judge to sentence him to hang, although the prosecution did not ask for the supreme penalty in his case.

Since Fleagle was a wealthy man and employed the best attorneys, appeals were taken to the supreme court of Colorado in his behalf, as well as for Royston and Abshier. On March 13, 1930, the supreme court sustained all three conviction and sentences and ordered that they be hanged the following week.

In a last effort to escape the death penalty, Royston hinted to the officers that if he were given life imprisonment, or the reward for the train robbery be given his wife, he would confess all his knowledge of the train holdups and implicate the others involved. But the court overruled this, and Royston went to his death without talking.

Although the other three bandits were now dead, the search for Jake Fleagle continued. It was learned that he had been in correspondence with a gambler, who was immediately placed under surveillance. The man confessed that Jake had asked him to participate in a "job" in Arkansas. The man had been communicating with him through the "personal" column of a Midwestern newspaper and it was arranged that an answer to Fleagle's request to meet him in Yellville, Arkansas, be inserted in the paper. Fleagle outlined the itinerary he wanted the man to follow in a letter. The officers then arranged for another advertisement in the newspaper setting a date for the meeting.

Post office inspectors, special agents of the Missouri Pacific Railroad and two Los Angeles detectives were on the passenger train upon which the meeting was to occur. Fleagle boarded the train at Branson, Missouri, about twenty miles from Yellville. He was recognized by the officers who immediately told him to throw up his hands. Answering, "Like hell I will!" he attempted to draw his gun and was shot by three officers simultaneously. Rushed to the hospital at Springfield, Missouri, an emergency operation was performed, but it was too late. Jake Fleagle, the leader of the gang calling itself the "Lamar Wolf Pack", died. Although conscious to the end, he refused to make any statement.

Thus the railroad police investigating the train robbery were responsible in part for cleaning up one of the most vicious groups of bank robbers operating in Colorado and Kansas. Yet, even with this gang disposed of, officers were now concentrating their efforts on other clues that would determine beyond a shadow of a doubt the responsibility for the train robbery.

XII

The Nobel Robbery

While plans were being completed for the arrest of Jake Fleagle, the Rodeo, California, branch of the Bank of Pinole was held up and robbed by bandits on September 26, 1929. During the holdup, off-duty Sheriff Arthur McDonald casually entered the bank. Observing masked men putting large quantities of bills in sacks, he drew his gun and immediately opened fire. He was greeted with a return hail of bullets and fell severely wounded, although continuing to fire until his gun was empty.

One of the robbers was seen staggering away, blood dripping from his side. However, the bandits had managed to scoop up $27,000 in currency. In his flight toward a waiting car, the wounded man dropped his Thompson submachine gun.

Later that day, the car in which the gang escaped was located in the hills above Berkeley. Considerable blood was spattered all over the front seat. Neighbors had noticed a blonde woman driving a brown sedan around the area where the touring car was later found. It was apparent the woman was the same as the one who drove the getaway car from the abandoned cement plant after the holdup of train No. 36 the preceding year. The robbers also answered the description of the men who held up that train. From fingerprints found on the machine gun and in the automobile, it was determined that Jake Fleagle was not one of them.

While working on the lead of the brown sedan, the officers received information from a tip that the man they sought was Frank Smith, better known as Frank P. Ellis. He had been seen in South San Francisco in a brown Hupmobile sedan, answering exactly the description of the getaway car used by the woman to drive the Rodeo bandits from the Berkeley hills. Ellis had made inquiries about the handling of payroll funds for the manufacturing plants of South San Francisco and apparently was going to hold up the messenger carrying a large payroll of $50,000.

The license number of the Hupmobile was obtained from the Department of Motor Vehicles in Sacramento and checking on the purchase of this car, the officers learned he had traded in a two-toned Overland coupe. On inspecting the coupe, the officers noticed how closely it fit the description of the coupe driven from the abandoned Cowell plant where the Hudson auto had been set on fire after the 1929 robbery. The rear luggage compartment was discovered to have been enlarged sufficiently for a man to conceal himself and a hole had been cut from the seat above this compartment to allow ventilation and communication between anyone in the compartment and the driver of the coupe.

After this discovery, every effort was made to locate Ellis and his associates. Persons known to be friendly with him were shadowed. The police met with little success, although it was learned that Ellis and his gang were responsible for the burglary of the Fresno Calwa Winery in March of 1928. Liquor valued at approximately $50,000 had been stolen. Also, definite proof was uncovered that the Ellis gang had robbed the post office at Tracy, California, of $26,000. Intensive investigation further developed that Ellis had a record for bank robbery in California, having served time in San Quentin from 1909 to 1919. It was also learned he had served a term in the Washington State Reformatory for burglary from 1922 to 1925.

While the search for Ellis was being made, train No. 36 was dramatically held up near the deserted station of Nobel, between Berkeley and Richmond, California, on the morning of November 7, 1930. Five bandits carrying machine guns, revolvers, and dynamite took part in a swiftly accomplished robbery that suggested a cool, daredevil gang.

As the train left University Avenue Station in Berkeley, the rear brakeman of westbound train No. 9 saw a man dressed in brown clothing climb onto the tender of No. 36. Since he believed the man to be a hobo attempting to beat his way for a ride, the brakeman paid no attention.

When the train was about a quarter of a mile down the track, where the right-of-way is near the Bay, and the easterly side is screened from the highway by a row of streets and factories, engineer Peter Lemery and fireman H. D. O'Brien were surprised by a man clad in brown overalls and wearing a white gauze mask pointing a pistol at them. Lemery was immediately instructed to stop the passenger train at a certain station, the name of which the bandit could not recall. Lemery asked if it were "Nobel." The bandit answered, "Yeah, that's it. It's coming up the line over there. That's where we want to stop." As the train slowed up to the station, the bandit gave the order, "Stop! Stop!"

When the fire in the locomotive was extinguished at the robber's instruction, Lemery and O'Brien were ordered to jump down from the engine on the Bay side and to walk around to the front of the engine. When they reached the front of the engine, they were made to sit down and told to behave themselves.

The two crewmen noticed a dark sedan parked outside the right-of-way near the fence and the man who had been guarding them moved over to a point between a string of flat cars parked on a siding. There were five members of the bandit gang, two guarding the rear end of the train, one who had forced his way into the mail car, one on the flat cars who took the packages thrown out from the mail car and the fifth man who acted as guard for the engine crew and passed the loot over the right-of-way fence near where the auto was parked.

The bandits had entered the mail car shortly after the train had stopped. Mail clerk John McClintock heard loud talking outside the car and then a terrific explosion which he figured to be a torpedo, although it proved to be nothing more than a rifle-shot into the side of the car. He went to the open window and saw three men with guns pointed at him, one of whom immediately demanded that he open the car or it would be blown up. McClintock opened the door and was instructed to jump down and climb onto the adjacent flat cars.

After looking into the car, one of the robbers called to McClintock to come back and get into the car. McClintock obeyed. As he climbed back into the mail car, the bandit asked, "Where's all the money?" The clerk queried, "What money?" The bandit's reply was in a determined and confident tone, "The money for Pittsburg and those other places!"

The clerk then pointed to a small bank package on a bench near a dozen registered pouches. Slitting the package open, the bandit noted the currency and threw it out to a member of the gang waiting on the track. The robber then found several bank packages for other small towns and threw them out also. McClintock stood motionless and watched the robbery, saying nothing. The bandit then turned to him and snarled, "You've been lying to me and I ought to kill you right now!"

When the robber, who appeared to be the leader and was familiar with the interior of the mail car, was satisfied he had obtained all the available loot, the clerk was ordered to turn his head while the bandit stepped from the

The Nobel Robbery

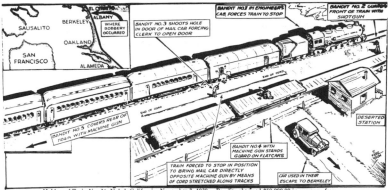

Holdup of Train No. 36, Nobel, California, November 7, 1930. Bandits obtained $50,000.00 in currency from mail car. No. 1, Charles Berta; No. 2, James Sargert; No. 3, Frank P. Ellis; No. 4, Edward J. Kenny; No. 5, E. R. Sherwood

Frank P. Ellis, alias Frank E. Smith

car. Signalling to his partners, the bandit led his men over to the automobile and sped away. Several passengers, as well as the engine crew, obtained the license number of the car, adding that all the bandits carried machine guns.

When police arrived, they immediately investigated the license plate number and learned the automobile was a Studebaker sedan stolen from an Oakland garage the previous night. Officers then discovered a sack containing 1,000 silver dollars which had been left on the ground adjacent to where the auto had been parked. It was debated whether the bandits had simply overlooked the sack, or considered it too heavy and bulky to handle. The other looted mail sacks were found a few hours later in Berkeley and that night the stolen Studebaker was located at Euclid and Virginia Streets, not far from where the Dodge touring car used in the Rodeo bank holdup had been abandoned.

Everyone's thoughts turned to Frank Ellis. The manner in which the crime was committed and the getaway style were typical of Ellis. And certainly Ellis would not have gotten involved with any loot less than $50,000.

It was discovered that in 1928 when Ellis had been issued license plates on the Overland coupe, he listed his address in care of his brother-in-law in Alameda, near Oakland. Working on this dramatic new lead, officers located Ted Lyda and questioned him intensively. Lyda identified a photograph of Ellis and said that Ellis had borrowed various amounts of money from him. That money was always repaid, but only after some dramatic bank or train robbery. The brother-in-law, a mechanic, admitted that the rear deck of Ellis' Overland coupe had been enlarged under his supervision. But he denied that he and his wife had any knowledge of Ellis' criminal activities. They always believed that Frank was an honest advertising man. After further questioning, the officers were given Frank's address.

That afternoon a posse consisting of railroad police

officers, post office inspectors, members of the Oakland and Berkeley police departments, United States Secret Service and representatives of the sheriff's office of Alameda County and district attorney's office of Alameda County, assembled at the Oakland post office. Plans were made to surround the cottage where Ellis was living and every preparation made to bring about his capture alive. But since he was a killer, officers armed themselves with tear gas bombs, machine guns, heavy rifles and revolvers. After a thorough rehearsal of the part each was to play, the posse proceeded to 103rd Avenue in Oakland where Ellis lived at 1944A, a small rear cottage.

Moving quietly, the officers divided into several groups and stationed themselves in various positions, some covering the rear of the house, others covering both streets, and the remainder approaching from the front of the house. One man rang the doorbell, the others standing aside. When Mrs. Ellis opened the door, she swung the door wide, inquiring what he wished. All three officers rushed into the house with their guns drawn. Deploying to different rooms, they were prepared to shoot it out. At first Ellis appeared not to be at home. Then it was noticed that the bathroom door was slightly ajar. When this door was pushed open, the officers found Ellis quietly sitting on the toilet with his pants down.

He was ordered to put his hands up, which he did immediately. The officers stationed at the rear of the cottage were called in, although the other groups were left in their positions in case other members of the gang called upon the Ellis'. A quick search of the cottage revealed two rifles, one .38 caliber automatic pistol, one .22 caliber automatic pistol, two pairs of handcuffs, two bullet-proof vests, a quantity of narcotics and hypodermic needles. In addition, officers found $400 in currency and several rolls of quarters.

The most vital piece of evidence discovered was a notebook belonging to Ellis, a notebook containing coded memoranda concerning train robberies. Payroll dates were found of various large manufacturing towns as well as the names and address of several men who turned out to be members of the gang. The notebook also contained a letter from a title company concerning a piece of property to be transferred from William Sherrod to Evelyn Sherrod, thus disclosing another alias used by Ellis. All the evidence was loaded into one of the autos and taken to the Oakland post office.

Ellis was placed in an automobile with chief postal Inspector George Austin and brought to the Oakland main post office. Mrs. Ellis accompanied her husband in a second police vehicle. When the auto drove into the post office yard and as Ellis was being walked toward the Seventeenth Street door of the building, he made a sudden dash for liberty. It seems that enroute to the post office, officers casually noticed a sedan bearing Washington license plates following the posse. This sedan came to a stop on the Broadway side of the building and when attempting to make his escape, Ellis ran around the corner of the post office in the direction of the sedan. His escape attempt was ended by a well directed shot from the pistol of secret service operative Leonard Schmidt. Ellis dropped to the pavement with a bullet through his stomach. Although rushed to the Emergency Hospital, he died an hour later without making any statement. In the meantime, no trace could be found of the sedan which had driven off when the shooting had started.

Mrs. Ellis was questioned immediately. She refused to even admit that the man, Ted Lyda, the officers contacted was her brother. When told her husband was dead, she demanded to be taken to the morgue to see his body. There, she felt the body of her husband and broke out in a laugh, stating that the body was still warm, he wasn't dead and the police were trying to trick her. She was taken to a cell in the Oakland City Prison.

Ellis' photograph was identified by rear brakeman

Heikka as being one of the robbers who held up train No. 36 at McAvoy on June 22, 1929 and Mrs. Ellis was positively identified as being the woman who drove the getaway car used in connection with the Rodeo bank robbery. All these identifications were made within 24 hours after the arrest of Ellis.

The information regarding the property being transferred from William to Evelyn Sherrod was furnished by the special agent of the Southern Pacific and post office inspectors in Portland. From this development, officers learned of a number of transactions in the stock market where Ellis using the alias of Sherrod lost $10,000 in a short while. A number of keys, apparently for safe deposit boxes, were found in the cottage. A check was made of all banks for safe deposit boxes under the aliases Ellis was known to have used. This led to the recovery of $6,000 from a safe deposit box in Oakland under the name Evelyn Sherrod.

Meanwhile, it was discovered that W. T. Mallahan of Seattle was married to a sister of Mrs. Ellis and special agent Coturri of the Southern Pacific contacted post office inspectors Imus, Pinkham, and Case in Seattle to question Mallahan. Although intensively questioned, Mallahan denied any knowledge of Ellis' actions. However, it was learned that William Mallahan and his brother James Mallahan both had criminal records extending over several years. Under further interrogation, he revealed that his brother James who was living in Los Angeles had traveled to Oakland with Ellis a few days after the Nobel robbery. James had written to him after this trip telling him that Ellis casually mentioned participating in the Nobel robbery and several other holdups.

James Mallahan was located in Los Angeles and arrangements were made for him to visit inspectors in San Francisco. He stated that Ellis arrived in Seattle the last time in November 1930, and while there visited several places paying off his debts. Ellis gave him $50 in five-dollar bills and took three packages of $500 each in five dollar bills out of his suitcase. The following day, Ellis invited Mallahan to join him for a trip to California, all expenses paid. Mallahan jumped at the chance and they met at the railroad station that afternoon.

Accompanying Ellis to Oakland, Mallahan learned a lot from the talkative Ellis. He mentioned that Ellis was quite proud of the severe wound he received in the Rodeo bank holdup and was able to survive. Once the train pulled into the Oakland terminal, the two men were met by a man known as "Charlie" who drove a blue Chrysler sedan and was accompanied by a woman who had a dog. Mallahan described Charlie as being short and dark. When shown a number of photos of suspects, he immediately zeroed in on Charles Berta. Berta was wanted in connection with several other serious crimes in San Francisco and Seattle.

Information had come in a few days before that several men in a blue Chrysler sedan had been stopped by the inspectors at the state and federal quarantine station at Hilt, California, during October 1930, and appeared nervous when a search was made of the auto. Inspectors found a metal case containing machine guns. The men in the car immediately tried to bribe the inspectors. Unsuccessful at this, the men pulled out pistols and sped away. Though a general alarm was given throughout Oregon, the occupants of the blue sedan eluded pursuit. However, the license number was obtained and this information was given the officers investigating the train robbery.

Upon checking the Chrysler bearing Washington license plates, it was discovered to have been sold to a party known as T. H. Ward. The salesman identified a photograph of Berta as being "Ward" and it was also learned the car had been purchased with a cashier's check secured by attorney John Garvin of Seattle. Garvin was immediately questioned and said he believed "Ward" to be a liquor runner. However, a short while later he informed the post office inspectors he had met "Ward" in Palo Alto in December of 1930 and that "Ward" was financing the defense of Mrs. Ellis. Confidential circulars bearing a photo of Berta were then distributed. When shown Berta's photograph, engineer Lemery stated it resembled very closely the man who climbed over the engine tank and held him up.

Berta had vanished completely. Friends could not contact him and police were frustrated. Then an informer tipped police that Berta, under the alias "York", resided in Oakland until December 1, 1930. Armed with this clue, police discovered that he had been assigned the laundry mark "506," which was later changed to "3250." This information was also circulated in a confidential manner and laundries requested to be on the lookout for a man whose laundry bore either of these numbers.

Meanwhile, the investigation of the names and addresses in code taken from Ellis' book bore fruit. It was learned that the notation "Esherwood, Trentonarms," had reference to the Trenton Arms Apartments in Seattle, where E. Sherwood had rented an apartment from October 29 to December 5, 1930. When the landlady of these apartments was permitted to look at a number of rogues' gallery photographs, she immediately identified the picture of Edward Shannon, a criminal of long record with various aliases. Shannon was indeed Sherwood.

Investigation in Oakland developed Sherwood registered at the Calfironia Hotel on December 1, 1930, checking out the following day. Before leaving the hotel, he had a bellboy send a heavy package to Seattle by express. This package was addressed to R. W. Carlton, Olive Tower Apartments, Seattle. With these new leads to track down, an attempt was made to discover where he was on November 7. A check of all transportation facilities determined that Sherwood under the alias "E. Miller" was a passenger on an airplane from Seattle to Oakland. Because of fog, this flight was diverted to Concord and the passengers brought to Oakland by taxi. His photograph was identified by fellow passengers and by the taxi driver. Another check was made of the California Hotel records and it was discovered that E. R. Sherwood had registered there on the morning of November 6 and that he checked out on the morning of November 8. Records of the West Coast Air Transport Company showed he returned to Seattle on the evening of November 8.

When crewmen and passengers identified Sherwood's photograph, there was no longer any doubt that he was a member of the Ellis gang. Furthermore, Ida Wilbur, a maid at the California Hotel, found a package after Sherwood left containing silver half dollars amounting to $195.50. Since the plunder obtained in the Nobel robbery contained considerable silver and nickels, this was the final link connecting Sherwood to the robbery.

Several weeks passed without trace of Sherwood, although it was believed he was somewhere in the Pacific Northwest. The first news of his whereabouts came from a suspicious grocer in Olympia, Washington. Two women visited the grocer's store and made a small purchase for which one woman paid with a roll of nickels. The grocer took the roll and was smilingly informed she had saved nickels in the amount of $84. He suggested she go to a bank and exchange them. Both women left and climbed into a Buick sedan with a Texas license plate. Since the woman said she would indeed cross the street to the bank, the grocer was suspicious and jotted down the number of the license plate which he called and gave the police.

In tracing the auto, the police found it had gone to Seattle and quickly organized a roadblock. The Buick was stopped on the outskirts of Seattle and two men and two women surrendered without resistance. They gave their names as E. R. Sherwood and R. W. Carlton. Immediately, they were arrested for questioning in connection with the train robberies at McAvoy and Nobel. Later that night, police officers searched the Sherwood apartment in Seattle and discovered a large supply of narcotics, as well as numerous rolls of nickels. In a drawer, $246 was found, plus 95 cents in nickels.

On Sherwood were found several safe deposit keys and within days, most of the Nobel loot was recovered. In the meantime, the federal grand jury in San Francisco had voted indictments charging Mrs. Ellis and Sherwood with being principals in the McAvoy and Nobel holdups. During this time, the search continued for Berta. A tip came in that Berta was hiding in a small Seattle apartment house. A check of every apartment was made under all his old aliases. As a result, Seattle detectives visited the Malloy Manor Apartments and asked to inspect an apartment which was being rented to C. W. Rogers and his wife who gave as their permanent address Oakland, California. A brief search satisfied them that they were in the right apartment and quickly stationed themselves across the hall to await the residents.

About 11:15 p.m. on January 26, 1931, Mrs. Rogers approached the front door to her apartment and was greeted by the two Seattle detectives. The woman explained to the questioning officers that she hadn't seen her husband for a week and did not know the kind of work he was in. But her evasive remarks satisfied the police they had the right woman, who answered perfectly the description of the woman known to be Berta's girlfriend. Officer James Fraser questioned her about the window shades, thinking that some signal might be conveyed to Berta. "Should they be drawn or left as they are?" he asked. "Just leave them as they are," she replied. At this moment, the telephone rang and the officers told her to answer it and be careful what she said. The conversation from outside was, "What's the trouble up there?" She replied, "Why, you don't want to come up here; you don't want this number; this is the wrong number. What do you want?" Without waiting for an answer, she hung up. About 30 seconds later, the phone rang again and the caller repeated the question, "What's the trouble up there?" She screamed into the phone, "Bill, get the hell away from here! The bulls are here!" The officers knocked the phone from her hands and rushed down the back stairway into the alley. From there, they ran out into 43rd Street. Officer Tom Carroll saw Berta standing by the corner of 43rd Street and University Way. Proceeding down the north side of 43rd Street toward the corner, while officer Webb crossed the street and walked down the south side of 43rd Street, they approached Berta. But spotting them coming toward him, he walked north on University Way at a rapid rate.

As the two officers reached the corner, Berta was standing about 25 to 30 feet from the corner near a university student in a cadet's uniform waiting for a bus. As the two policemen closed in on him, Berta pulled the cadet in front of him and Officer Carroll who was carrying a sawed-off shotgun could not get it into action because of the danger to the cadet. Carroll made a quick jump, caught hold of Berta's right arm and at the same time noted a small box in Berta's right hand. Carroll said, "The jig's up, Berta, we're the police." Berta screamed, "Help! Help! This is a stickup!" A uniformed policeman on patrol rushed up to the scene and the detectives explained who they were. Officer Tweet joined in subduing Berta who was battling firecely with the men. Officer Webb had secured hold of Berta's left arm which he allowed Tweet to grab and hang onto. But Berta pulled his right arm from Carroll and at the same time kicked Carroll's feet from under him. The officer scrambled to his feet and got behind Berta, pinning the latter's arm behind him and bending him forward. In this position, Berta's hands came together and he screamed, "I've got a surprise package for you, you son of a bitch!" Carroll shouted to the other two officers, "Look out he's got a gun in that box." Berta managed to discharge two shots from his gun. But because of the position in which he was being held, the shots landed in the pavement. Webb then shot Berta in the right shoulder and the bandit offered no further resistance.

On examining this gun, it proved to be a .38 caliber Smith and Wesson with a six-inch barrel. Berta also had on him a .38 caliber automatic pistol on a .45 caliber frame. In his pockets were several cartridge clips for the automatic. Both Berta and the woman were booked at the city prison and Berta received treatment for his shoulder wound which was not serious.

Since the San Francisco Police Department was seeking Berta in connection with the murder of officer John Malcolm during a holdup, the Seattle officers were undecided whether they should surrender Berta to the U.S. marshal on the train robbery charge. But when it became evident that Berta would undoubtedly be convicted of train robbery and had a fair chance of being acquitted on the murder charge, he was surrendered to the U.S. Marshal on January 31, 1931.

Two or three days later, the final incriminating evidence linking Berta to the McAvoy and Nobel holdups was found. Two suitcases hidden under some bushes on the isolated shores of Lake Washington were accidentally uncovered, yielding a .30 caliber Remington rifle, two automatic pistols, two rifles, a Thompson submachine gun, a bullet-proof vest, and the expensive clothing of a man with the laundry mark "506." The Oakland laundry owner positively identified Berta as "Mr. York" who had traded there a few months before. Berta was scheduled for trial before the U.S. Commissioner.

While police were checking on Berta's associates in Seattle, information was received that a gangster named Edward J. Kenny with whom Berta was particularly close was the fourth bandit in the holdup. Kenny was known as a gunman for various liquor runners in the East. A check on his movements showed that he was on the Pacific Coast at the time of the Nobel robbery. A number of circumstances were discovered in connection with Kenny that clearly indicated the information was correct and he was the fourth bandit. A description of his automobile was obtained and circulated quietly and on one occasion the car was sighted by the driver of a mail truck in Seattle who immediately gave chase. But Kenny escaped and headed for the East Coast that same day.

On April 28, 1931, Mrs. Ellis and Sherwood were tried jointly in the United States District Court in San Francisco before Judge Louderback upon the charges of robbing train No. 36 at McAvoy and conspiracy to rob the train at Nobel. The prosecution was handled personally by United States Attorney George Hatfield. Mrs. Ellis was represented by attorney Nathan Coghlan and Sherwood by attorney Joseph Sweeny, both considered among the leading criminal lawyers on the Pacific Coast.

The prosecution used 56 witnesses. It was proven that Sherwood purchased the tickets at Bay Point and boarded the train with another man. Also, Mr. and Mrs. Ellis attempted to purchase dynamite in Pleasanton on June 20, 1929, but failed. The two then broke into the storehouse at the quarry and stole a large quantity of dynamite.

In all, the witnesses drew a chain of identification and circumstantial evidence around the two defendants and the case went to the jury late on the afternoon of May 4, 1931. The jury was out only 50 minutes, returning a verdict of guilty for both. Judge Louderback then promptly sentenced each to serve 25 years in federal prison.

On June 12, 1931, police in San Francisco learned that Edward Kenny had been machine-gunned by rival underworld figures in Camden, New Jersey, for attempting to establish a white slave racket without the approval of the gangland leader in the area.

Berta's trial began on August 27, 1931, before Judge Kerrigan in the United States District Court in San Francisco. One hundred and twenty-nine witnesses and 36 pieces of evidence were submitted to the jury. The outstanding witness was a 15-year-old boy who lived in El Cerrito and who played truant from school on the day of the Nobel robbery. He testified that he was hunting ducks and observed an automobile near the right-of-way fence before the train came along. Three or four men were un-packing machine guns. He testified that Ellis and Sherwood were two of these men and described the third man as a Spaniard with a pointed nose. He noticed the auto was a Studebaker sedan. One of the men spotted the inquisitive boy and told him to run along. At that, the boy took a good look at the men and watched one move articles around in the back seat of the car, articles that sounded as if they were guns, tools, and duck decoys. He concluded his simple and direct testimony by describing how the train stopped opposite where the auto was parked, but did not see the actual holdup because all the action took place on the opposite side of the train. With engineer Lemery identifying Berta as the bandit who held him up (his mask slipped slightly during the robbery and he had an opportunity to observe his features), the final link was forged and the case went to the jury.

On September 19, 1931, the jury returned a verdict of guilty after deliberating 93 minutes. Berta then received a sentence of 25 years to be served in the federal penitentiary at Leavenworth, Kansas.

While the trial was in progress, evidence developed that the fifth man was James Sargert, known as "California Eddie." Sargert was an intimate friend of Kenny and had a reputation as a desperate holdup man. He was wanted at that time by the New Jersey authorities for murder. When shown a photograph of Sargert, the 15-year-old witness immediately identified him as being the man who he had described as "Spanish looking, with a pointy nose." With that, circulars were developed announcing the usual reward of $2,000 for his arrest and conviction.

In October 1931, an informer wishing to collect the reward tipped the police that Sargert was in Portland. When this story was investigated and appeared to be correct, it was decided to send the informer with post office inspector George Austin and assistant special agent Guilfoyle to Portland.

After arriving in Portland, the informer made contact with Sargert in a boardinghouse occupied by a group of underworld figures. A posse was quickly formed to storm the old three-story house in Portland's skid row. When the final assault arrangements were completed on the afternoon of November 5, 1931, it was decided to make the raid later that night. The house was kept under surveillance until about 10:30 p.m. when a posse consisting of railroad police officers, post office inspectors, Oregon state police, and Portland police surrounded the hideout. Because of city ordinances, the actual raiding party was commanded by Lieutenant Pat Molony of the Portland police. Entry was easily gained, and Sargert, along with Mabel Wakefield and an auto salesman named Ivan Quirk who had supplied the gang with several automobiles, were arrested.

Sargert appeared before the United States Commissioner in Portland on November 30, 1931, at which time he waived extradition hearing. On December 1, United States Judge Fee signed the order removing him to the jurisdiction of the United States District Court in San Francisco.

While waiting for trial, Sargert was positively identified by Carl Brown who lived in the house on the front of the same lot on which Ellis' cottage was located as being one of a group of men who visited Ellis on Sunday, October 26, 1930, just prior to the train robbery. He was also positively identified by fruit inspector Barton as being the youngest of the men who accompanied Berta in the Chrysler Sedan at the time the machine gun was found. Barton had no difficulty in picking Sargert out of a line-up of prisoners. The 15-year-old youth also had no difficulty in identifying Sargert in the flesh.

On February 5, 1932, the jury found Sargert guilty on two counts of robbery of the mail train and conspiracy with the others to rob the train. He waived delay in passing sentence and Judge St. Sure sentenced him to serve 25 years in the United States penitentiary on the first charge.

After Sargert's trial was completed, railroad authorities breathed more easily. A great piece of work had been done. Now there remained the distribution of the reward. Soon, new claimants for a portion of the large reward appeared on every hand. It became necessary to conduct a thorough investigation of the claims made by each person wanting a share in the rewards and this investigation of the claims made by each person wanting a share in the rewards and this investigation was as extensive as is necessary in solving many crimes. Though the Southern Pacific Company had offered a reward of $2500 for information leading to the arrest and conviction of each person involved in the holdup of train No. 36, it was decided to distribute the reward on the same basis as the government rewards.

While this investigation was in progress, word was flashed from the U.S. penitentiary at McNeil Island that Sargert had escaped. All persons on the Pacific Coast known to be friendly with him were immediately placed under surveillance. Railroads and highways in the vicinity of McNeil Island were kept under close observation. However, Sargert was located on the island on April 18th, 1932, hiding under some building materials.

Sargert was not the only member of the gang to attempt escape. On December 11, 1931, Berta, with six other inmates who had secured rifles, captured the Leavenworth warden and used him as a shield as they literally blasted their way out through the main gate.

Although the convicts separated after the prison, their trails were followed. Three inmates were found dead in a house near the prison after a lengthy gunfight with the pursuing guards. Realizing they could not escape from the house, the three killed each other rather than return to prison. After a running gunfight in a nearby field, Berta was captured. Earl Thayer, notorious member of Al Spencer's gang of Oklahoma highwaymen and mail robbers, managed to reach the city of Leavenworth where he was quickly apprehended.

Sargert was tried on a charge of attempted escape from McNeil Island in the United States District Court in Tacoma in February 1933. Although acquitted on this charge after a bitterly contested court battle, he made another daring attempt to escape while being led away from court. Breaking away from the grasp of the marshals, he dashed down two flight of stairs in the Federal Building and out into the street. While racing down an alley, he slipped and fell on the wet pavement which dazed him enough to be captured.

Since the Department of Justice decided to convert Alcatraz Island into a prison for such escape risks, Charles Berta and James Sargert were transferred there in 1934.

With the dissolution of the gang it was felt that the most daring, resourceful, and successful group of robbers to operate on the Pacific Coast had been disposed of. In the two train robberies their booty amounted to approximately $70,000 of which about $52,000 was recovered by the officers. In addition, other crimes definitely traced to Ellis and his satellites showed they had obtained over a quarter of a million dollars. Ellis was without question a cool, determined leader, masterminding each case before attempting the robbery. After perfecting his plan, he gathered the most trusted assistants he could find. In most ways he differed from the usual gangland boss. After his various crimes he quietly paid off any debts he owed and returned to gambling in the stock market. He was a quiet man who shunned publicity and no one would have suspected him as a gangster. During the intervals between robberies, Ellis seldom visited resorts or hangouts that might be frequented by other gang leaders or holdup men. Without question, his story is one of the most dramatic in the history of western train robberies.

Photo Credits

Wells Fargo Bank History Room: vi, 4, 6, 8, 11, 13, 19, 37, 44, 54, 57 (bottom), 58, 59, 64, 66, 69, 81, 82, 83.

San Francisco *Chronicle* Library: 3, 28, 34, 49, 112, 126, 144, 161.

Central Pacific: 5.

Nevada Historical Society: 15.

Southern Pacific: 30, 40, 46, 55, 57(top), 75, 77, 86, 87, 89, 94, 95, 97, 98, 99, 100, 101, 102, 105, 106-107, 108, 109, 110, 121, 122, 133, 138-139, 140, 141, 142, 143, 147, 149, 153, 167, 169, 177.

Union Pacific: 154.

Federal Bureau of Investigation: 185.